HBR Guide to
Leading Teams

Harvard Business Review Guides

Arm yourself with the advice you need to succeed on the job, from the most trusted brand in business. Packed with how-to essentials from leading experts, the HBR Guides provide smart answers to your most pressing work challenges.

The titles include:

HBR Guide to Better Business Writing

HBR Guide to Building Your Business Case

HBR Guide to Coaching Employees

HBR Guide to Finance Basics for Managers

HBR Guide to Getting the Mentoring You Need

HBR Guide to Getting the Right Job

HBR Guide to Getting the Right Work Done

HBR Guide to Giving Effective Feedback

HBR Guide to Leading Teams

HBR Guide to Making Every Meeting Matter

HBR Guide to Managing Stress at Work

HBR Guide to Managing Up and Across

HBR Guide to Negotiating

HBR Guide to Networking

HBR Guide to Office Politics

HBR Guide to Persuasive Presentations

HBR Guide to Project Management

HBR Guide to
Leading Teams

Mary Shapiro

HARVARD BUSINESS REVIEW PRESS

Boston, Massachusetts

Copyright 2015 Harvard Business School Publishing Corporation

Library of Congress Cataloging-in-Publication Data

Shapiro, Mary.
    HBR guide to leading teams / Mary Shapiro.
        pages cm
    ISBN 978-1-63369-041-7 (alk. paper)
1. Teams in the workplace—Management.   2. Leadership.   I. Title.
    HD66.S4844 2015
    659.4'022—dc23

                                                          2015007184

ISBN: 9781633690417

eISBN: 9781633690424

What You'll Learn

How often have you sat in team meetings, grousing to yourself, "What a colossal waste of time. Why does it take forever for us to make a simple decision? What are we even trying to *achieve* here?"

Dysfunctional teams are maddening—and sadly, they seem to be endemic to organizational life. But as the team leader, you have the power to change things for the better. It's up to you to get people to work well together and produce results.

How do you avoid the pitfalls you've experienced so painfully in the past? This guide offers step-by-step advice, drawing on time-tested principles, practical exercises, guidelines for structured team conversations, and examples from a range of industries and organizational settings.

You'll get better at:

- Picking the right team members

- Cultivating their skills

- Setting clear, smart goals

- Rallying support both within and outside the team

- Fostering camaraderie and cooperation

- Addressing bad behavior before it gets out of hand

- Promoting healthy dissent

- Resolving conflict when it rears its head

- Holding members accountable to one another, not just to you

- Keeping them focused and motivated to the end

- Identifying best practices for your next team

Contents

Introduction   xi

Invest in the "people" side of teamwork.

Section 1: BUILD YOUR TEAM'S INFRASTRUCTURE

1. Pull Together a Winning Team   3

   Make it small and diverse.

2. Get to Know One Another   11

   Connect in a meaningful way and learn what people need to do their best work.

3. Establish Your Team's Goals   25

   Define your tasks and outcomes—and your processes for achieving them.

4. Agree on Individuals' Roles   35

   Decide who will do what on the team.

5. Agree on Rules of Conduct   45

   Specify how the team will operate as a unit.

Contents

6. Set the Stage for Accountability   55

Sort out how the team will enforce its goals, roles, and rules.

7. Commit to a Team Contract   67

Summarize what you've agreed to in your team-building conversations.

Section 2: MANAGE YOUR TEAM

8. Make Optimal Team Decisions   73

Create an environment where everyone participates.

9. Hold People Accountable   87

Build skills—and trust—in giving and receiving feedback.

10. Give People Recognition   99

Motivate them to contribute more by acknowledging what they've done.

11. Resolve Conflicts Constructively   103

Get problems out in the open right away so you can move past them.

12. Welcome New Members   117

Discuss what's working and what may need to change.

13. Manage Outside the Team   123

Cultivate mutually beneficial external relationships.

Section 3: CLOSE OUT YOUR TEAM

14. Deliver the Goods   133

*Keep everyone focused and working
productively until the end.*

15. Learn from Your Team's Experiences   139

Reflect on what worked and what didn't.

Appendix A: Rules Inventory   147

Appendix B: Cultural Audit   153

Appendix C: Team Contract   157

Index   *161*

About the Author   *165*

Introduction

Whether you're taking over an existing team, launching a new one, or have been leading a group for a while, getting people to work together to produce excellent outcomes is not easy. Each team is different, and each poses a distinct set of challenges. Maybe you've just been assigned to chair a task force of people from different units to launch a companywide initiative. Perhaps you manage five people who have to work together daily as a part of ongoing operations. Or maybe you've been struggling at the helm of a team so mired in conflict that the members couldn't reach agreement on anything if their lives depended on it. No matter what type of team you're leading, you probably face tight deadlines and high expectations and feel the pressure to churn out project plans, assign tasks, and, above all, execute.

It's only natural. We create teams to accomplish work, after all, so we tend to focus mainly on tasks. But that's just one side of the equation; we also need to focus on the *people* who will be carrying out those tasks.

If your team members don't have good relationships with one another, your team won't do good work. People will squabble. They won't trust each other. They'll feel underappreciated, grumbling that others aren't carrying their share of the load. They'll stop collaborating. Tempers will flare—and productivity will grind to a halt.

It takes time and energy to prevent complications like these and to get team members working well together. You have to explain tasks clearly, coordinate efforts, motivate people, resolve conflicts, give feedback, and develop skills. In short, you have to manage the people with as much discipline as you manage the work.

Before investing all that effort, consider whether you even need a team to do the job at hand. We've all been on teams assembled for the wrong reasons—to rubber-stamp an already-made decision, for example, or to spread out the risk and blame in case a project goes badly. To ensure that your team has a solid reason for being, conduct a straightforward cost/benefit analysis: Will it help you meet your goals and improve your outcomes? Or can you do the work just as well yourself, with greater efficiency and fewer headaches?

If you decide the investment is worthwhile, you'll want to create a *winning* team, of course—not one that crashes and burns or limps along indefinitely. This book will help you do just that. Effective team leadership unfolds in three stages: build-up, managing, and closing out.

Stage 1: Build Your Team's Infrastructure

Just like a house, a solid team needs a strong foundation. But instead of stones or cement, your materials will be early discussions about goals, roles, rules of conduct, and the metrics you'll use to gauge progress. Once you've enlisted people with the required skills and perspectives, the group must explicitly agree on what it's trying to achieve, how it will get there, and what success will look like. This is how team building really works. It's not about ropes courses or whitewater-rafting trips, it's about reconciling individual temperaments and work styles to get the most out of each contributor and the team as a whole.

You may be thinking, "Who has time for all these conversations? We have a job to do, and we're already in a pinch to get it done." But agreeing on *how* you'll do that work beforehand will make it go more quickly and smoothly. You'll have fewer conflicts to navigate, decisions to revisit, and tasks to redo.

Because each group has its own quirks, you'll need to build this infrastructure every time you create a new team—and every time you lose or add members.

Stage 2: Manage Your Team

If you've ever led a project, you know what it takes to manage tasks: You acknowledge when they're done well and on time. And when something misses the mark, you stipulate changes to get it back on track. Throughout the project, you strive for continuous improvement.

The same principles apply to leading a team. When people exhibit useful behavior—such as warning others before a deadline slips—point it out. This motivates them to keep it up and reminds others of what they should do to support team goals. It's just as important to nip negative behavior in the bud—a team member stops participating in meetings, for example, or verbally attacks those who disagree with her. Just as you monitor and tweak tasks to follow a project plan, keep a close eye on how people are doing relative to the goals, roles, and rules you've all agreed on—and talk openly about problems as soon as they crop up.

It sounds simple, but most team leaders don't do this. Instead, they let issues go unaddressed until someone explodes in frustration, or until everyone mentally checks out, bringing work to a standstill.

Stage 3: Close Out Your Team

Say you're almost ready to turn your prototype over to engineering, for example, or to present recommendations to the board of directors. You should be elated, right? The team is so *close* to achieving its goals. But you've noticed that people are skipping meetings or spending time on other work. What's happening?

When the finish line is in sight, team members often lose their focus, drive, and patience. They start thinking about the *next* project or obsessing about all their other work that has piled up. You may feel the same impatience to move on. Now more than ever, it's critical to motivate team members—and yourself—to wrap things up properly and capture best practices to apply next time around.

That's what this third stage is about. If you solicit your team's input on what went well and what didn't, you'll manage those problems better in the future. You'll grow as a team leader—and your team members will improve their own skills.

We'll cover each of these stages in this guide. Throughout, I provide sample structured conversations and activities developed from my experience of more than 20 years of consulting with teams. I draw on many real examples (some of them disguised) to show how team leaders have applied the advice in a range of situations.

You may feel uncomfortable with some of the activities, at least initially, since they deal with the "people" side of teams (an area where many leaders struggle, especially those who were promoted because of their technical expertise). But give them a try. I've seen them work for new and existing teams, large and small, colocated and virtual, and in just about every organizational setting—including financial services, manufacturing, customer service, technology, nonprofits, and government agencies. They'll help your team to grow, prevent and fix hard problems, and produce the results you're after.

Section 1
Build Your Team's Infrastructure

Chapter 1
Pull Together a Winning Team

If you've ever led a team, you've dealt with maddening members: Those who dominate meetings. Slowpokes who analyze every problem from every angle when the schedule is tight. Those who harp on reasons *not* to support decisions the group made months ago. Quiet folks who say nothing in meetings, but then complain endlessly at the coffee station about decisions that were made in their presence. Those who compete for "resident expert" status without actually contributing much at all.

You may have wondered: Do they stay up all night thinking of ways to torment me? What's wrong with them? Why can't they be more like *me?*

That's a common—though a bit melodramatic—response to the challenge of leading a team of diverse individuals. Socially we all gravitate toward people who are like us—those who understand our humor, enjoy doing the same things we do, and don't get offended when we cancel at the last minute (after all, they do it, too). Sameness minimizes conflict and misunderstanding. Yet, to paraphrase U.S. gum maker William Wrigley Jr. when two people think alike on a team, one of them is redundant. Assemble a team of people who are just like you, and you'll undoubtedly experience less frustration. The group will reach decisions more quickly, and members will approach the work in the same way.

[handwritten margin note: also 'if you are smartest in room']

But lack of diversity has a serious downside. If everyone on the team prefers big-picture thinking, who comes up with the practical steps necessary to realize the group's vision? If everyone likes taking risks, who plans a soft landing before you leap? Who handles the tasks you don't like to do or can't do well?

Research repeatedly shows that greater diversity on a team yields more innovation and higher-quality work. That's why each individual on your team should bring some unique combination of expertise and skills that will help you produce great work (see figure 1-1).

To achieve the diversity "sweet spot" you're aiming for, you must first envision the results you want, and then determine what strengths and capabilities you'll need to achieve them. If you're building a business case, for instance, you'll need expertise in data mining and proposal writing. Tap your network for people who are good at those things or ask your colleagues whom they'd recommend. Once you've got someone on board who possesses a critical skill, don't add another team mem-

FIGURE 1-1

Making the most of diversity

Use this list of task- and people-related strengths to determine what mix of knowledge and skills your team requires.

To complete the tasks at hand, you may need members who bring:	To get everyone working well together, enlist members who excel at:
• Relevant functional expertise (for example, in engineering, accounting, marketing, finance, or customer service)	• Facilitating meetings
	• Building consensus
	• Giving feedback
• Relevant industry knowledge (for example, in manufacturing, technology, health care, or financial services)	• Communicating in groups
	• Resolving conflicts
	• Negotiating
• Technological skill	• Motivating others
• An appetite for research	• Exercising emotional intelligence
• The ability to mine and analyze data	• Influencing others
• A knack for writing and presenting	• Networking with people outside the team who can provide resources

ber who excels at the same thing. Remember to address both task-related strengths and people skills when assembling your team.

Consider this hypothetical example illustrating the value of diversity on a team.

Imagine that your company has experienced a dramatic increase in products returned from customers. If you pull together a team of six engineers to analyze the problem, chances are they'll quickly come to one conclusion and make a recommendation consistent with their common backgrounds: It's an engineering issue, and the solution is to rework the design.

I know this is a cliché, but it applies here: When everyone on your team is a "hammer," then every problem will look like a nail, and every solution will be to pound it. Outcomes will be quick, consistent, and harmonious—but not innovative.

Now suppose you add people from customer service and marketing to your team. Team members will look at the problem from different viewpoints. Maybe it's an engineering problem, maybe customers don't understand how to use the product correctly, or maybe they're buying the wrong model for their purposes.

That's the good news—a variety of perspectives expands the number of possible solutions. But the team still must work together to come up with a single creative solution. The decision making takes much longer, and relationships may get strained as members hash out conflicting ideas.

So what's the right amount of diversity? Jon Katzenbach and Douglas Smith define the optimal makeup of a team in their classic *Harvard Business Review* article "The Discipline of Teams" this way: "A small number of people with complementary skills who are committed to a common purpose, set of performance goals, and approach for which they hold themselves mutually accountable."

Building on this definition and drawing on my years of experience consulting with teams and leading my own, I've developed the following principles for assembling an effective team:

Make It Small

The larger the team, the more difficult it is to find meeting times, the longer it takes to make decisions, and the tougher it is to manage information and work flow. So bring together the smallest number of people necessary to provide the skills and perspectives you need. That's usually somewhere between three and seven members. Other contributors who will be needed only occasionally—organizational allies, content experts, and advisers—should not be included as full-fledged members: That just wastes everyone's time. Instead, consult them at specific points and assign one member to serve as a conduit of information back and forth. For example, a finance representative should weigh in as you put together a budget request for a project, but that person obviously shouldn't participate in all the team building and ongoing work that doesn't require financial expertise.

If you are assuming leadership of an existing team, you'll need to start by deciding whom to keep and whom to cut loose. If the numbers feel bloated, consider defining a core team of a few essential people and moving others onto a "support" team that you enlist on an ad hoc basis. This strategy is particularly useful if you have inherited some noncontributors, complainers, or obstructionists. If you can't eliminate them, you can at least marginalize their impact.

Incorporate Skills and Knowledge

List the skills and types of expertise you'll need to tackle the team's responsibilities—not just what's needed to accomplish the work but also what will facilitate collaboration. (Again, use figure 1-1 to get started.) Then identify the fewest number of people who can cover most of those requirements.

You can also conduct this inventory to reevaluate your current team. If certain members aren't contributing much, ideally you'll remove them. But if you don't have that authority, try giving them "support team" status as suggested above. Does your team lack key competencies? Add people to fill those gaps—or at least identify advisers you can call on periodically.

Include Diverse Approaches to Work

The best teams offer a mix of work styles: people who carefully address one task at a time and those who can multitask, folks who excel at contingency planning and those who nimbly adjust when problems strike, and so on. Here, we're talking about people's natural inclinations, not the skills they've acquired through training or experience. When assembling your team, consider how people differ in their outlooks, priorities, and attitudes about decision making, change, and risk.

Don't drive yourself crazy trying to include every conceivable work style on your team. It's just not possible. But identify people whose wiring differs from your own and who possess characteristics essential for your team's success. If you're leading a team that will drive deep change in the organization, you may want members on both sides of the "change" spectrum: early adopters to generate creative ideas and late adopters to anticipate sources of resistance (see figure 1-2).

FIGURE 1-2

How are they wired?

When you're selecting team members, think about how they're naturally inclined to act. On each dimension below, most people will gravitate toward one end of the continuum or the other when they're on "autopilot," though they can adjust their behaviors with effort—when under deadline pressure, for instance.

	OUTLOOK	
Is detail oriented		Focuses on the big picture
Focuses on the next project deadline		Looks one to three years down the road
Decides on the basis of data	DECISION MAKING	Relies on intuition
Decides deliberately with analyses and contemplation		Decides spontaneously
Is a late adopter of trends; prefers certainty and clarity	CHANGE	Is an early adopter; is comfortable with uncertainty
Prefers incremental change; builds on what works		Prefers large, sweeping change; likes a "clean slate"
Places task completion ahead of relationships	PRIORITIES	Places relationships and harmony ahead of tasks
Focuses on the tasks themselves		Focuses on how the work gets done (the process)
Prefers a slow and methodical environment	WORK	Prefers a fast and fluid environment
Works on one task at a time		Multitasks
Spends time analyzing and preparing for risk	RISK	Faces risk with minimal planning
Identifies all possible outcomes and generates contingencies ahead of time		Prefers to make real-time adjustments as needed

Though work quality will benefit from a mix of personalities and approaches, relationships may suffer. For example, the big-picture thinkers might regard the detail-oriented people as data geeks crippled by "analysis paralysis." And the detail people may dismiss the big-picture folks as unrealistic or people who "shoot from the hip." *Team of rivals ...*

Why would you want both types on your team? Imagine how much work would get done with only big-picture thinkers to execute ideas. Probably very little. They'd generate lots of excitement and creative thought, but the goals would keep changing and expanding, and no one would focus on how exactly to accomplish them. And you wouldn't be any better off with an entire team of detail-oriented colleagues. They'd provide clarity, structure, and solid documentation of progress—but their outcomes would probably resemble what's been done in the past. They wouldn't break new ground.

So the differences are worth the potential headaches. We'll talk more about how to handle the conflict—both destructive and beneficial—that is a natural by-product of diversity in chapter 11, "Resolve Conflicts Constructively." But let's now look at ways to minimize the headaches by anticipating some of the problems members will have.

Chapter 2
Get to Know One Another

Now that you've identified the skills and expertise your project needs and pulled together your team, it's time for your launch meeting. You've made a PowerPoint deck outlining the project. You've provided coffee and donuts, and everyone's sitting around the table expectantly. How do you begin? If you're like most of us, you welcome everyone, introduce yourself, and then ask each person to share his or her name, title, and maybe "a little about yourself."

But hang on. Don't zip past those introductions. Before you dig into that deck and start explaining and organizing tasks, it's essential to gather some personal data to help the group establish effective goals, roles, and rules of conduct. I'm not suggesting that your team members should share their favorite reality TV shows or "fun facts" about themselves. Rather, I'm encouraging you to connect with them in a meaningful way so that you—and the rest of the group—will know what each person needs to do his or her best work.

Begin by addressing the fundamental questions they're privately contemplating while munching on their donuts:

- Why am I on this team, and what are your expectations of me?

role clarification

- Why are others on this team?

- How do you see us working together?

If your team members understand why you chose them, they'll have a clearer sense of how they can contribute. And just as important, they'll learn what other team members bring to the table. You're also helping people recognize from the outset the purpose for the team's diversity, so they'll be less likely later to snipe about how some members "leap before they look" and others can't "analyze their way out of a paper bag." By naming differences from the beginning, you're acknowledging the need to work across them and highlighting the value each person brings.

Having everyone say "Hi, my name is Ellen, and I'm from St. Louis" doesn't accomplish any of that.

As the team leader, you've intentionally chosen people with complementary skills and perspectives. Now you need to shed light, in a series of group conversations, on members' personal strengths, work styles, and priorities.

Personal Strengths

Each member's skills, knowledge, and work style will add to the pool of valuable team resources. A simple way of getting the group up to speed on those resources is to go around the room and ask individuals to share what strengths they bring to the team and what others say they do well. Because many people are reluctant to talk about themselves, you may need to prompt them with a structured conversation (see, for example, the sidebar "Artifact Exercise").

You can also invite them to talk about one another. For existing teams or for members who have collaborated before, ask people to complete this sentence about each colleague: "In the past, I've relied on this person to . . . ."

Then it's your turn to speak up: Say why you placed each individual on the team and what contributions you expect each member to make.

One project leader at a large pharmaceutical company did this in a quirky way: He cut a poster of his business unit's logo into jigsaw-puzzle pieces. At his team's first meeting, he explained why he'd asked each person to participate, handing him or her a puzzle piece as he did so. Then he had the seven members assemble the puzzle.

You may be thinking, "There's no way I can do that—it's too hokey." And that might be true for your team. Members have to be receptive for this to work, but when they are, it packs a punch. The team leader in the example above had enough seniority that people were willing to suspend disbelief and give the exercise a fair

ARTIFACT EXERCISE

Before meeting as a group for the first time, ask each team member to come prepared with a five-minute story about a past accomplishment. This can be a personal or business achievement—anything the storyteller is proud of. Have everyone bring an artifact (some physical object, whether it's a photo, a diploma, or a rock from Mount McKinley) that symbolizes the achievement.

When people share their stories in the meeting, prompt them to describe the opportunities or challenges they faced, the actions they took, and the outcomes they produced. Then debrief by asking the team:

- What was your reaction to hearing everyone's stories?

- What do these stories tell us about the skills that each person brings to the team?

It's never too late to do this exercise, even with existing teams or those you inherit. People are often amazed by their colleagues' accomplishments. The stories may uncover hidden resources the team can put to use. They also give members a chance to communicate their own strengths and help them appreciate one another.

One manager at a government agency found this exercise particularly helpful when she was tapped to lead a team of account managers and engineers. She knew she had to neutralize a lot of pent-up mistrust—not a small feat—because the two groups had a long history of organizational conflict. They didn't like or work well with each other.

So she used the artifact exercise. By listening to team members' stories of achievement, each group gained a new appreciation for the other's challenges. It took time to break down the long-standing barriers between them, but this exercise gave them a good start. It opened their minds so they could find new, better ways of working together.

shake. He also articulated a clear goal for doing it: He wanted to convey that everyone's voice had equal weight, even though the scientists in the group outranked the administrators and junior members in the corporate hierarchy. It was an important point to make, because the team's ability to produce meaningful recommendations for the company depended on the full commitment and engagement of all its members. The scientists got the message that, at least on this team, they had to collaborate with their junior colleagues. And the junior folks felt empowered.

Work Styles

Some of your team members may prefer a "divide and conquer" approach, where you break projects into small tasks and have people work independently on their sections, with limited interaction until it's time to assemble the final report. Others may prefer to work together in all aspects of the project, believing that collaboration generates a better outcome. Not surprisingly, the first group will probably feel micromanaged if forced to work with others constantly, and people in the second group will feel isolated if left on their own for too long.

By finding out how individuals prefer to operate, you and the team can develop rules that enable all members to contribute meaningfully (see chapter 5, "Agree on Rules of Conduct"). Yes, the "divide and conquer" members will have to collaborate occasionally, and the "let's stay joined at the hip" members will have to work independently at times. But understanding those conflicting preferences helps you and the team anticipate members' needs and determine how to work together productively.

So how do you figure out individuals' preferences? In a meeting, have each member talk about prior team experiences. This allows people to learn how their teammates naturally behave when deadlines loom and stress increases. Ask everyone:

- What was your best team experience and why? What made it so good? What did team members or the leader do that made it such a good experience? What was the atmosphere like?

- What was your worst team experience and why? What made it so bad? What behaviors drove you crazy?

Another approach is to have each team member complete a diagnostic like the Myers-Briggs Type Indicator. People's traits—how decisive, detailed, intuitive, or adaptable they are—have an impact on their behavior and on how they'd prefer to operate on your team.

You have many diagnostics to choose from (see the sidebar "Personality and Work Style Assessments" for a few examples). The goal in using any of them is to help people on your team understand their own traits and styles and recognize how other members differ. This sets the stage for the team to craft a "team style" of working.

Such diagnostics are powerful partly because they reinforce the notion that people's intentions are generally good and that the way they behave isn't random, arbitrary, or malicious. Rather, their behavior reflects what makes sense to them. It may not make sense to others until people can more clearly see the motives behind it.

That's what happened with Nancy, a nurse at a community-based health care center where each patient is assigned a team: a physician, a nurse practitioner, several nurses, and a patient care manager. Whenever Nancy met with a team to determine a patient's care, she asked lots of questions because she preferred to make decisions on the basis of abundant data. However, team members with different styles misinterpreted her

PERSONALITY AND WORK STYLE ASSESSMENTS

Myers-Briggs Type Indicator

Indicates how people get their energy (working alone or working with others), how they make decisions (using intuition or data), what they base their decisions on (emotions or objective information), and how they manage their lives (with or without structure).

Howard Gardner's Multiple Intelligences

Recognizes different types of intelligences beyond standard IQ, which measures only logical and mathematical intelligences. Teams benefit when they bring additional intelligences (linguistic, musical, kinesthetic, intrapersonal, interpersonal, and spatial-visual) to bear on their work.

DISC

Identifies the level of dominance (control of environment), influence, steadiness (cooperation), and conscientiousness (accuracy and completeness) each member brings to the team.

Big Five Personality Test

Assesses individuals' extraversion (how outgoing or solitary they are), agreeableness (how cooperative or not), conscientiousness (how organized or casual), openness (how curious or cautious about diverse people and experiences), and emotional stability (how steady or impulsive).

motives. The physician thought Nancy saw herself as smarter than her teammates; others assumed she didn't trust them to make good decisions.

It wasn't until the team did a personality diagnostic that they discovered what really drove Nancy's behavior. She scored much higher on conscientiousness and the need for detail and control than the other team members. And most of them scored higher than she did on valuing relationships. With their focus on maintaining harmony in the group, they were reluctant to bring up dissenting ideas when making decisions together. They usually agreed to the first idea offered and didn't ask people to explain their opinions, fearing that disagreement would be seen as a challenge. Nancy, whose assessment revealed a focus on tasks rather than relationships, didn't view questions and disagreement as personal attacks. She saw them as tools for making the best decision.

Unnamed, these differences between Nancy and her teammates had created a big problem. But now when Nancy asks a lot of questions, the rest of the team understands that it's just how she operates—and that her questions may actually prevent errors.

Priorities

It's also critical to identify up front where the team ranks on each member's personal priority list. This is particularly true for ad hoc teams, where you're given a limited amount of time, and you're adding work to people's already-full plates. It's also important when you've borrowed team members from their "real" jobs, because they're now accountable to you *and* their managers. As

ALLAYING FEARS ABOUT ASSESSMENTS

As helpful as diagnostics can be, they make some people feel exposed or vulnerable. To put them at ease, you can:

Make It Optional

Allow members to opt out. The team needs to be OK with that and to understand that people differ in their need for privacy.

Explain the Purpose

If people understand that the results will help the team define its goals and ways of working together, they'll be more receptive to the exercise. Remind them that these assessments are *not* evaluative or judgmental—it's neither good nor bad to be identified as decisive, for instance, or collaborative. Rather, effective assessments simply describe individuals' traits, increasing self-awareness and others' understanding.

Emphasize Confidentiality

Assure team members that you won't share results with anyone outside the group, and set the expectation that no one else will, either. The insights are for the team's use only.

Let Members Choose What to Share

If people don't feel comfortable discussing individual results, that's all right—you can still get value from reviewing results in the aggregate. But if they're willing to disclose what they've learned about themselves, ask how they think their colleagues scored and have them explain what behaviors they're basing their conclusions on. People usually guess others' styles correctly, as you can imagine. That member who loves to create PERT charts for projects? Of *course* she scored high on conscientiousness. And the person who loves to deliver presentations? He probably scored high on extroversion.

Discuss Impact on the Work

Ease people into sharing their experiences. If you're leading a small team, give them time to think before they speak. If it's a larger team, you might group them according to their styles. That way, they can trade stories with similarly wired members before opening up to the whole team. Someone might say, for example, "I scored high on introversion. That explains why I usually gravitate toward task management. I love making sure the hundreds of moving parts are in alignment. However, because I'm an introvert, I have a hard time asking others for input. I prefer making decisions alone and sometimes miss important points as a result."

When you break into small groups, you can also ask people to discuss what they need from a team to do their best work, what they like about teams, what

(*continued*)

(*continued*)

they struggle with, and how they define a good team member, leader, and meeting. Gathering this kind of data now will help the team figure out its rules and processes later.

Collect Results in a Chart

Create a visual to show members where they overlap and where they differ. You can match traits with names or just indicate how many team members have each tendency. Even if you do the latter, names often come up as people discuss the diagnostic, guess one another's styles, or talk about themselves. Either way, it's useful to discuss which traits the team has in abundance and which it lacks. For new teams, consider how the distribution of styles might shape what the group is likely to do well and what it might overlook. For existing teams, ask what impact the various styles have had on group dynamics (both positive and negative). The health care team, for instance, found it enlightening that Nancy was the only one who scored high on conscientiousness. No wonder her behavior frustrated the others—she was an outlier.

Emphasize Value Added

Have people with similar traits brainstorm in small groups—that way, they'll come up with a long list of all the good things they bring. Then ask the groups to

share their lists with the rest of the team. This helps
people appreciate the value of having different styles
in the mix. For example, those who love big, sweep-
ing change are more likely than others to challenge
the status quo and prompt innovation. Conversely,
those who prefer small, incremental adjustments will
prevent the team from making changes too hastily or
without due cause.

you assembled the team, you probably negotiated for the
amount of time each ad hoc member would give. But
even your full-time members have personal (and often
invisible) limits to their availability.

For that reason, a group conversation about individuals' priorities yields useful information for all types of
teams. Members come with their own goals, ambitions,
and outside commitments. So ask how many hours they
can realistically devote to your team every week. Also
get them to specify competing demands on their time.
Sometimes I have each member draw up and share a
rough pie chart showing how they'll allocate their time
across their multiple commitments.

By finding all this out early, you can make smart assignments that align with individuals' priorities and availability. While this may not seem like a fair way to distribute the work, it's the right way. The team's outcomes will
be only as ambitious as its members' availability allows.

And the team can boost its performance and avoid missing deadlines by funneling more tasks to members with more time and a greater level of investment.

Beware the usual expectation that everyone will participate equally. This is unrealistic and sets everyone up for disappointment. Expecting equity also hurts performance, since members who give the work a lower priority may do just what's minimally required. And it hurts members for whom the work is a *high* priority: They aren't given as much responsibility as they'd like, and they may feel they have to scale back their contributions to the lowest common denominator. Instead of looking for equal participation, expect members to contribute to the best of their abilities.

Once everyone has a clear sense of what each member brings to the team and how individuals' styles and priorities differ, you're well positioned to establish the team's goals, roles, and rules of conduct, which we'll cover in the chapters that follow.

Chapter 3
Establish Your Team's Goals

No matter what kind of team you're leading, the group must set two types of goals: *Task goals* specify what your outcomes should look like. They direct *what* gets done, defining the work of the team. *Process goals* describe the team's approach to working together. They direct *how* individuals do the work and interact with one another. (You'll work out the "how" in more detail when you create rules of conduct, addressed in chapter 5.)

Although it's tempting to skimp on the goal setting and immediately start planning tasks, taking the time up front to develop both task and process goals yields several benefits:

- Group decision making becomes clearer and more efficient—and conflicts are easier to resolve. The team can cull its options by asking, "Which ideas move us closer to our goals?"

- Individual members approach autonomous decisions consistently. This allows for a smoother discussion when people report back to the group, and it expedites the team's progress.

- Goals provide a framework for holding team members accountable. When giving feedback (positive or negative) or evaluating a team member's performance, you can answer the question: "Did this outcome or behavior support our goals?"

Let's take a closer look at both types of goals.

Task Goals

Suppose you've been asked to lead a team to plan how your company will store and ship products during warehouse renovations.

First, you need to agree on outcomes—your task goals. To develop them, ask members to describe what an optimal future would look like. Have them envision the warehouse layout, for instance, and the staffing. Also consider as a group what failure would look like. Often, people can easily articulate what they *don't* want; recasting their language reveals what they would like to see happen. Finally, discuss the desired customer experience from beginning to end.

During this conversation, your team may decide, for example, that the final plan should include the fewest possible moves (of people, equipment, and inventory), a way of updating all affected departments on progress to facilitate their planning, a continual feedback loop to permit real-time adjustments, and sufficient procedures and staffing to keep the renovation process invisible to customers. Once you've got those overarching goals in place, the team needs to define three components:

Actions

What steps will the team take to achieve its task goals? Teams often rely on one or two members with project management skills to create and present a plan, which others then add to or revise. However you develop it, any plan should include key activities, contingencies, checkpoints for monitoring the work, guidelines for keeping stakeholders informed, and details about who needs to sign off on which steps.

Deadlines

When will the team take each step? Without deadlines to drive you forward, the actions you've planned will remain a wish list. Work backward from the final due date, and estimate (realistically) how long each step should take. Allow buffer for actions outside the team's control, such as waiting for go-aheads from senior management.

Metrics

How will the team measure progress on its tasks? What are the criteria for completion? Clear measures of team success will help individuals understand what's expected of them and how they'll be evaluated. You may want to gauge financial performance (reduced costs, for example, or increased margins), productivity (reduced time), or quality (reduced errors). Metrics should spur team members to work hard and "stretch"—but they'll discourage people if they aren't within reach. And they need to be specific so that team members won't interpret tasks differently ("What do we mean by 'accurate' reports?").

Process Goals

Clear process goals allow you to blend individual team members into one cohesive unit, so these goals are every bit as critical to your success as planning the work. Most teams don't even bother with process goals—they assume they already know how to work together. But remember all the diversity you purposely embedded in your team? Each member probably has a different understanding of how to collaborate, not to mention different styles and preferences.

Identifying process goals requires that you define the team's culture. You'll explicitly address the following questions:

- **What will it feel like to work with the team?** Will it be inclusive with shared responsibility or dictatorial with autocratic decrees? Will there be mutual respect or backstabbing and political alliances? Will the tone be optimistic or pessimistic? Supportive or competitive?

- **What will the relationships look like?** Will they be equal or hierarchical? Open or closed? Trusting or suspicious? Social and personal or all-business?

- **What do we want from those relationships?** Do
  we want to simply get the tasks done or develop
  longer-term connections? Divide and conquer
  tasks with minimal interaction or learn from and
  mentor one another?

- **What do we value?** Do we care more about speed
  or accuracy? Risk taking or compliance? Innovation or building on core strengths?

Of course, no team in the universe *tries* to establish
a culture of suspicion, backstabbing, and passivity. But
we've all been on a team like that. A team's culture
evolves whether you talk about it or not—so it's better to
spell out what you're aiming for, giving people the opportunity to explicitly reject undesirable behaviors. Otherwise, you're likely to wind up with a culture that evolves
by itself in the wrong direction—one, for example, where
people stop contributing because they see only a few individuals getting all the credit, or one where the mantra
is "CYA."

It's important to incorporate members' personal goals
into your team's process goals. Otherwise, people may
act against the group's interests to satisfy their own. Say,
for instance, that one member is eager to gain visibility
with senior leaders. It's best to know that *before* he de-
cides to leak messy work-in-progress details to a stakeholder over lunch. (You can prevent that sort of problem
by creating a "team of equals," where all members get
visibility and credit, not just the team leader.) But how
do you uncover his personal agenda? You'll need to read
between the lines. If you asked, "What do you want to

get out of this team project?" he would never say, "More visibility to advance my career." But he might reveal that objective through his questions ("Who will get to present the final proposal to senior management?") or through his comments on what success or failure would look like ("We need to be seen as innovators in the company").

There's no set formula for creating process goals beyond focusing on behaviors and the feelings they elicit, but here's an example of what process goals can look like.

At a large Midwestern college, the Student Life Department faced deep resource cuts and needed to figure out how the team could do more with less (including fewer people). Group members developed these process goals to guide them:

As a team, we aspire to:

Support each other fully. *We will understand and appreciate one another's lives, both at work and outside of work. We will create a climate where team members feel free to ask for help, offer help, and listen.*

Communicate fully. *We will share information and best practices; we will share what we do at work and in our lives, to better support one another; and we will share our successes to motivate ourselves and position our team to build upon those accomplishments.*

Be innovative. *We will develop a climate where it feels safe to take risks (including expressing ourselves) and experiment, and where downsides are identified but upsides are protected from naysaying.*

Those process goals enabled the new team of 10, down 30% from its original size, to do the hard work of deciding which programs to keep and which to cut, and to put in the longer hours needed to maintain most of its regular programming. One academic year later, the director was pleased to see that all 10 staffers were still on the team; she had not lost a single member to burnout.

So how can you get the conversation about process goals started? Ask members to recall the best and worst team experiences they shared when getting to know one another. Call out common themes, and build your goals around them. Usually the "worst" stories are the most vividly told. They also powerfully convey what problems people don't want to encounter on the new team.

If you used a diagnostic tool to highlight diversity when building your team, revisit the results. Not surprisingly, people's personality traits will influence the types of relationships they want with team members and what qualities they value in a team setting. Once again, group individuals according to their traits, and ask each subgroup to propose a set of process goals. Then, as a full team, negotiate goals that work across diverse traits.

Usually, you'll want process goals to accommodate most people's preferences, on the theory that individuals contribute most effectively when they feel comfortable. In the example mentioned earlier, the goals of the Student Life Department reflected its members' high interpersonal intelligence (from Howard Gardner's Multiple Intelligences diagnostic). But sometimes it's good to go against the grain and set process goals that stretch people and build future capacity. For instance, if most members shy away from conflict, your team may set a goal of engaging in rigorous discussions, encouraging constructive dissent, and seeking honest feedback.

Process goals should tap into team members' aspirations as well as their styles. Here are two exercises for doing that:

Capture ideals

Ask each person to prepare a one-paragraph e-mail that he or she would like to send to a friend, at the close of the project or initiative, about the team's fantastic experience working together. When you meet, have members share their hypothetical e-mails and identify themes. These idealized visions of the future can inform both task *and* process goals: What do people want to accomplish? How do they want to accomplish it?

Channel hopes and concerns

Have each member write down two hopes for the team and two concerns. Discuss these as a group, again looking for areas of overlap. Often one person will articulate something as a hope and another will frame the same thought as a concern. For example, "I hope we'll work efficiently together" is equivalent to saying, "I'm concerned that the project will take much longer with us working as a team than it would if we tackled the tasks individually." For both statements, the theme is making the best use of everyone's time. Translate common themes into three to five process goals for the team. To continue with the example above, one process goal might be, "We will work efficiently and respect everyone's time."

This exercise can be effective even for large groups. Consider how well it worked for a regional nonprofit that brought together about 60 people to build a new program strategy. The team included representatives from the staff, the nonprofit's board of directors, and other organizations with overlapping missions, as well as current and potential funders. To decide how they would work together over a series of several weekends, each person was asked to submit by e-mail two hopes and two concerns for the sessions. The hopes of all 60 people were compiled into one list, the concerns into another—with no indication of who said what.

On their first weekend together, the team members divided into 10 working groups. Half of the groups received the list of hopes; the other half, the list of concerns. Each group chose up to five themes from its respective list and posted them on a flip chart. The full group of 60 then looked at all 10 charts and went through the same process of identifying three to five recurring themes. After doing so, the team broke into groups again and crafted the themes into goals.

In about two hours, then, 60 people agreed on five process goals defining how they would work together.

Once you've established process goals, keep reinforcing them. State them at the beginning of each team meeting or reflect on them at the meeting's close (answering

"What did we do today that advanced our process goals?"). Consider including them as a footer in every team e-mail or posting them in office common areas. These reminders prevent members from reverting to old behaviors and drifting from the team's agreed-upon way of operating.

At the same time, though, consider the process goals a set of living principles that will evolve as team membership changes and people develop their team skills. To keep these goals salient in a changing environment, periodically review them by asking, "Which ones have we accomplished? Which ones are still priorities? Which should be more ambitious, or less so?" Conduct this review at least quarterly and at your project or initiative's end, as you're gathering lessons learned to apply to the next team experience.

Chapter 4
Agree on Individuals' Roles

Once you've set task and process goals, establish the roles that each member will play. That includes your role, too: You may have the title "leader," but what does that mean—to you and to the rest of the team? Even though everyone has worked on teams before, each individual will bring different ideas about leadership to *this* team. Some people may expect you to make all decisions unilaterally and tell them what to do. Others may expect you to lead the team in making decisions together and build consensus on who will handle which activities.

To prevent confusion, you must have an explicit conversation about who will do what on the team. (Here, we're talking about "internal" roles, essential to producing solid work together. In chapter 13, "Manage Outside the Team," we'll look at "external" roles for managing relationships outside the team.) Each member needs to know what his or her role is and what it means to succeed in that role. Without that discussion, some members may jump in and take on tasks that don't have clear owners—and some may see that "initiative" as grabbing power, or at least overstepping boundaries. By agreeing explicitly on who has what responsibilities, teams avoid misinterpreting motives, duplicating effort, and fighting turf battles.

You've already considered roles in terms of expertise. When assembling your team, you chose people because of what they can do, whether it's computer programming, for instance, or managing vendors. And you've already shared, during introductions, what kind of expertise each individual brings to the team (see chapter 2, "Get to Know One Another"). But here are two other ways to define roles in teams:

- **By structure:** Most teams have a basic structure of one leader and multiple team members. The leader has one role to play; each of the members, another.

- **By activity:** The team must complete many activities to reach its goals. For example, someone will plan the project; someone else will keep senior management informed. Each of those activities constitutes a role.

You can take either approach to frame the group's discussion about roles. One way is not any better than the other. The same is true for how roles are distributed. You can match roles to strengths or, conversely, give people opportunities to stretch. Growth assignments will mean more work for you because of the monitoring and coaching they require, but they can help you develop new competencies in your people.

Defining Roles by Structure

To clarify which behaviors people can expect from the leader and which they can expect from team members, try completing the form in table 4-1 as a group.

As you capture and discuss everyone's input, you'll expose differences in thinking. Work together to reconcile them. You might, for example, ask each team member to write down five behaviors of a good team member, and

TABLE 4-1

Clarifying behaviors

Leader	Team members
Here's what I propose to do as the leader:	Here's what we propose to do as members:
Here's what I need from you as members:	Here's what we need from our leader:

five of a good team leader, and then have people share what they wrote. Identify points of agreement, and use those to establish basic roles for you as the leader and for your team's members.

Another useful exercise is to lead the team through developing a "job description" for the ideal team member, as if you were going to post an ad to attract strong candidates.

When teams do this, they often list obligations such as those in table 4-2.

Your team will need to define each obligation to ensure consistent understanding: For instance, what does it mean for members to "pull their weight"? One way of clarifying expectations is to ask each person, "What would you need to *see* to know that someone is pulling his or her weight?" Team members may suggest specific behaviors, such as volunteering for new assignments or offering to assist others who are not meeting deadlines.

At a large pharmaceutical company, a "client express" team (assembled to improve communication between customers and account managers) wrote a job description for its members. After the group spent hours crafting it, one person observed, "There is no human being alive capable of meeting all those requirements!" Rather than feeling that they'd just wasted a lot of time creating something that wasn't doable, team members realized that they needed to prioritize their job requirements, which helped them set more reasonable expectations for themselves.

It's critical to explicitly define leader and member roles if you're on a team of peers. When no one has for-

TABLE 4-2

Defining expectations

Regarding:	Team members are expected to:
Task work	• meet deadlines • keep everyone informed on progress • meet targets
Relationships	• manage their own emotional responses • maintain good working relationships • resolve conflicts
Collaboration	• pull their weight • accept and support team decisions
Meetings	• attend all required meetings • come prepared • actively participate
Time management	• give advance notice before pushing back a due date • return all team-related e-mails, texts, and calls by close of business each day

mal authority, teams are often tempted to decide, "We don't need a leader. We can all share that role." Although that can work, most leaderless teams find that tasks take longer, the quality of the work is lower, and more conflicts arise among members.

Instead, consider rotating leadership throughout the project. For example, during data collection, the team's analytics expert might act as the leader. When it's time to create the final report for stakeholders, the person with the best writing skills might assume the role.

However, it's usually a good idea to designate an overall leader, as well. You'll want someone to maintain a big-picture view of the team's work (both task progress and relationship dynamics) and to serve as a tie breaker when the group has a hard time making a decision.

Defining Roles by Activity

Teams that define roles by activity often divide them into two essential categories: those that manage tasks (focusing on getting the work done) and those that manage processes (making sure members work well together). See table 4-3 for an example.

When looking at all these roles, you'll quickly see that you, the team leader, can't do them all. Think about what happens at just one meeting: Perhaps you take up the facilitator role to guide the team through all the agenda points you want to cover. While you're doing that, you can't also play gatekeeper, devil's advocate, and consensus taker.

To distribute roles, make assignments based on what you've learned about members' strengths and natural tendencies, or allow people to volunteer for what they would feel competent doing. Either way, people's dominant traits often indicate what roles they'd do well and enjoy. For example, Myers-Briggs "judgers," who need structure and order, can make great project managers or note takers. Extroverts, who get their energy from working with people, may prefer the liaison role.

Team members can fill multiple roles simultaneously or over time. For example, if Janice is detail oriented and good at organizing, she may play project manager in the beginning, shift to note taker and goal/rule keeper as

TABLE 4-3

Defining roles

Task roles	Process roles
Meeting facilitator: puts the agenda together, leads the discussion, and makes sure the meeting starts and ends on time	**Gatekeeper:** pays attention to who is and isn't talking; invites quiet members into the conversation
Project manager: sets up the project sequence and timeline; holds members accountable to that plan	**Mediator:** names conflicts (often the "elephant in the room") and then guides conflict resolution
Task specialist: organizes and leads a portion of the larger project, such as conducting the research or doing the analysis	**Devil's advocate:** challenges the team's thinking to increase rigor in decision making
Note taker: records all key decisions; documents the progress of the team	**Morale manager:** keeps members energized by remembering birthdays, organizing social events, and so on
Liaison: informs stakeholders (clients, boss, customers) about team activities; brings their ideas and concerns back to the group	**Consensus taker:** monitors the commitment level during team discussions to see if people really agree with decisions
	Goal/rule keeper: monitors adherence to team goals and rules; facilitates ongoing "continuous improvement" discussions

specialists step in to manage different aspects of the project, and then come back as project manager at the end to tie everything together and capture lessons learned.

The roles your team needs may evolve. When one team's leader announced his retirement, the group created a new role: succession planner. That person became responsible for working with the retiring leader to capture his institutional knowledge before the team lost it.

Periodically ask, "Are our roles still working for us?" If they aren't, the team may need to redefine them or change who does what.

Reconciling Individual and Team Interests

No matter how you clarify roles, it's important to recognize a dilemma that's central to teamwork: balancing each person's need for control and autonomy (including your own) with the team's shared goals and accountability. Why is that difficult? Because members will be evaluated on what the *team* produces, not what they do on their own. Their reputations (and future opportunities for assignments and promotions) may suffer if the team doesn't produce good work. No wonder team members often want to do it *all* themselves and micromanage one another.

To work together productively, they need to trust that their teammates will do a good job, and they must accept that the team's outcomes will differ from what they would have done individually. They need to feel ownership and pride in those joint outcomes—yet they also need the autonomy to perform their individual tasks as they see fit. Otherwise, they'll throw up their hands and say, "Why bother working hard? You're just going to redo it anyway."

You can avoid frustration and prevent duplicated or discarded work by creating clear boundaries. Within those boundaries, give members control over their own tasks. Spell out what can be done autonomously within each role and what needs approval by others inside or outside the team. Decide when progress reports for each role are required, and in what format, so the team feels assured that tasks will be accomplished on time and according to specifications. Also specify opportunities for team members to weigh in on someone else's decisions or actions. For example, before any subgroup goes off to plan a task, the whole team might brainstorm about it and suggest performance metrics. And then the subgroup can use this input—or not.

You may occasionally have to "invade" the boundaries you have so carefully defined. That becomes easier if you've clearly articulated the criteria for success within each role: When individuals fail to meet certain standards, you can simply redistribute their delegated responsibilities. Suppose one member of your team is responsible for synthesizing customer data collected by the group. Say you've specified how the report should be structured and how much secondary research to include, and you've set expectations for accurate numbers, solid grammar, and correct spelling. If the first, and certainly the second, draft doesn't meet those criteria, give the role to someone else.

With the team's goals and roles established, you've agreed on what the team seeks to accomplish and who will be responsible for which activities. You're now ready to craft the team's operating rules, which map out how the team will work together.

Chapter 5
Agree on Rules of Conduct

If you ask six team members what they think "completing work on time" entails, you'll probably get six different answers. The same holds true for your team's other aspirations.

Now that you've talked openly about roles, the group shares a broad understanding of what a good team member is. But you must also sort out what a good member *does*—that is, the rules that will guide everyone's behavior.

We each have our own rules of conduct, of course. Yours may tell you that getting to a 9:00 a.m. meeting at 9:03 is just fine. Or that it's OK to chime in mid-presentation when you're enthusiastic about an idea. Or that you should remain silent to avoid rocking the boat when you disagree with a decision the majority of people seem to support.

So what happens when you work with someone who thinks that a 9:00 start time really means 8:55? And that interrupting is rude? And that silence signals agreement? One or both of you end up frustrated, angry, or feeling disrespected, and tensions will mount.

Generally speaking, people want to do a good job and work well together. But when individuals' rules of conduct are unspoken, motives are often misinterpreted ("He's just doing that because he always has to be right" or "She's trying to hog the spotlight").

Rules of conduct build on the team's process goals (see chapter 3, "Establish Your Team's Goals") to clarify how you'll make decisions, keep everyone informed, run meetings, play nicely, hold one another accountable, assess progress, and continually improve.

Here's an example: An executive committee at a large pharmaceutical company had a reputation for behaving territorially and bad-mouthing each other. When a new chair took over, the group established an important new goal: "We will project a unified sense of mission and strategy across silos." The committee then identified a few rules of conduct to guide members' behavior:

1. Support the team's final decisions, even when you would have made a different call.

2. Express your support when communicating decisions to constituents.

3. Share decisions with stakeholders, but keep the discussions that led to them confidential.

The chair relentlessly held members accountable to these rules. As a result, when the company announced a reorganization of its regional offices, there was no finger-pointing or back-channel griping, and executives in lower ranks said they noticed a more collegial tone at the top.

Teams often skip discussing rules of conduct for the same reason they tend to gloss over process goals: They assume their members all know how to work on teams. Yes, they all do, but they do it *differently.* For example, some may be accustomed to having an agenda for every meeting, while others find agendas restrictive for short meetings, say, or brainstorming sessions. The purpose of discussing your team's rules isn't to determine the *one right way* of running a team. It's to agree on the *one consistent way* you'll run this particular team.

Rules of conduct:

- Clarify what others expect of you, the leader.

- Make members' behavior more predictable.

- Rein in members' behavior so you won't have to play "cop" as often.

- Reduce the amount of time you spend rehashing processes, such as how team decisions are made.

- Provide criteria for objective feedback and conflict resolution.

Like process goals, rules of conduct will form and evolve whether you talk about them or not. Without deliberate conversations, you'll find that unproductive rules crop up as people mimic what you and other influential team members do in practice. If you, the leader, routinely show up five minutes late for meetings, lateness becomes the norm, overriding any notion that punctuality is important. Rules also evolve according to what you reward. By listening to a team member complain about another member, you reward that behavior—you're giving the complainer your attention. And that kind of exchange becomes an accepted way of operating, even if the team originally agreed that members should try to resolve conflicts without your intervention.

Get your team members thinking about rules by asking them, "How do you want to handle X?" (fill in the blank with meetings, conflict, delegation, feedback, and so on). If they've completed a personality diagnostic, have them work with people with similar styles, and reframe the question: "According to your style, what is the best way to handle X?" This allows them to ask for what they want in an objective, nonpersonal way. It also brings different ideas to the surface, none of them "wrong." The team can discuss their respective merits and then agree on one way.

Reconciling personality and style differences isn't the only reason to create rules of conduct (though it's a big one). If you're leading a cross-unit team, you'll need to blend the different approaches. If you've added new people to a team, you'll have to take their perspectives into account. If you're managing two teams that must collaborate to achieve larger goals, you'll have to establish a third, overarching set of rules. You get the picture:

Any time you bring people together, you have to create explicit rules of conduct—or the work will suffer.

Here are a couple of exercises to help your team establish its rules.

Begin with a Boilerplate List

Rather than having open-ended discussions about desired conduct—which can take a lot of time and exhaust everyone—use an existing framework. For example, the Rules Inventory in appendix A lists basic rules for respect and trust; meeting discussions and decision making; dissent and innovation; feedback and reporting; and conflict resolution.

A framework like this serves as a starting point for establishing your team's top 10 rules (a manageable number to generate and remember). You can then reach agreement on them through what's called the *nominal method of decision making:*

- Ask individuals to do their own assessments: Which rules has the team followed from the get-go? Which would they like to add? Which would they rate as their top 10?

- At a meeting, post everyone's lists on the wall.

- Have team members walk around, view everyone's lists, and put checks next to the 10 rules they value the most (with fresh ideas in the room, their picks are likely to differ from their original 10).

- The rules with the most votes become the team's top 10.

49

This exercise works well for new and existing teams. At a large technology retailer, a team of eight Service Center staffers had worked together for several years, but they had never held team-building conversations. As a result, some counterproductive rules of conduct had emerged: For instance, team members weren't following up on customer requests. As more and more of those requests went unaddressed, people started pointing fingers. The team decided it was time to create explicit rules of conduct; members consulted the Rules Inventory and worked together to come up with the following list:

1. Bring up problems (regarding tasks or relationships) when they arise. Don't expect them to go away; instead, name the "elephant in the room."

2. Take ownership and follow through on problems.

3. Don't let things fall through the cracks. Even if the next step is someone else's responsibility, stay in touch until it's done.

4. Tell people what you need. Don't expect them to guess.

5. When responding to someone's request, always explain why you are doing what you are doing, especially when you have to say no.

6. When asking for something, always explain why you are making the request. This allows the person to come up with an alternative solution if what you are asking for isn't possible.

7. If you need training or tools in order to be successful, ask for them.

8. Take risks, but inform key people so that they don't get blindsided. Analyze the risks, identify the unexpected consequences, and plan for them.

9. Think Center-wide. When your actions diverge from usual practice, always ask, "What impact will this have on the team?"

10. Start each meeting with individuals sharing "what I did this week that constituted excellent customer service."

To make these rules stick, the team regularly reviewed them, especially when they experienced backsliding. And when the Service Center added three employees, veteran staffers used orientation as an opportunity to reexamine the rules. They invited the new hires to propose different rules or suggest changes to existing ones.

Even if the makeup of your team doesn't change, members should periodically reassess its rules. As with goals and roles, you can do this quarterly or each time you close out a project. That keeps the rules relevant as tasks and timelines change. It also helps quash undesirable behaviors that emerge, as the Service Center staffers discovered.

Conduct a Cultural Audit

A cultural audit helps newly blended or ongoing teams with new members identify rules of conduct that already exist—whether explicitly established or unofficially evolved. The team can then decide what to keep, modify, discontinue, or add.

A few days before you meet, ask people to think about how they would describe to a new member "the way things are done around here." Use the following questions as prompts:

- What rules were you told explicitly when you joined the team? Did someone take you aside and give you the "inside story"? If so, what did that person say?

- What rules do you *wish* you'd been told about early on?

- Has a teammate ever told you, "That's not how it's done around here"? (Violating an unknown rule is often the quickest way to learn!)

- What criticisms have you heard about others' behavior? Name the criticisms but *not* the people involved.

As the leader, conduct your own audit of the culture. Don't spend too long on it: Your spontaneous responses are probably the most accurate. (To prompt thinking, see appendix B, "Cultural Audit," for a list of behaviors.) When the team meets, ask members to share their perceptions. Take time to highlight differences—they're often a source of conflict (or at least confusion). As in the Rules Inventory exercise, ask members to vote for the top 10 rules they'd like to see the team adopt.

A team I consulted with at a large health care company used the Cultural Audit to identify and resolve a culture clash. The leader, a VP of marketing, had brought together some internal folks and a group of contractors to create a social media campaign. But the two camps had problems gelling. The internal folks complained that the consultants were too lax about details and deadlines, and too informal. Not surprisingly, the contractors saw the company insiders as bureaucratic and stodgy. When each group fell back on its own home rules, conflicts arose. The Cultural Audit gave the team a nonjudgmental way of recognizing the two sets of rules, which took the heat out of the conversation. Members then negotiated one common set of rules to guide interactions within the blended team.

Rules of conduct should help your team work together smoothly and productively, so keep things simple and practical. Focus on behaviors that will improve collaboration and the quality of the work. Early on, though, it's usually best to err on the side of more structure (and a few more rules), which you can adjust or relax as the team hits its stride. For instance, you might start out with a rule about answering e-mails by the end of the day. As that behavior becomes ingrained, you may no longer need that rule to ensure responsiveness. When teams don't have clear, specific rules at the outset, they often have to impose structure later as confusion and conflict arise, which takes more time and energy than spelling out desired behaviors in the first place.

You'll find more suggestions for rules when we cover decision making (chapter 8, "Make Optimal Team Decisions") and accountability (chapter 9, "Hold People Accountable").

Chapter 6
Set the Stage for Accountability

"Step into my office . . . I have a little feedback for you."

If you're like most people, that sentence strikes fear into your heart. You expect the worst: bad news. A pink slip. The end of life as you know it.

Understanding how it feels to be on the receiving end is part of what makes giving feedback to *others* so hard. But providing it is an essential part of your job as team leader. It's how you ensure that the work gets done on time, on budget, and according to quality standards. It's how you sharpen people's skills and keep them motivated. It's how you demonstrate commitment to their development and recognize their efforts to grow.

To all those ends, you must monitor tasks against project plans and track people's behavior against the team's process goals, roles, and rules of conduct. You may find the task-monitoring side easier, but you'll achieve good outcomes on tasks only if team members work together productively.

Say you've got one team member who holds forth during meetings. That violates a team rule—"Share airtime"—yet no one calls her on her behavior. Instead, people roll their eyes when she starts talking, cross their arms, and hunker down for a long, irritating meeting. If this dynamic continues, you'll end up with lots of frustrated and silenced members—and poor decisions.

Better to correct the behavior before it gets out of hand. Hold people accountable by reminding them of the rules for working together that everyone agreed on. When that troublesome team member starts pontificating, you can say, "Let's follow our rule of sharing airtime and give someone else a chance to comment."

The good news is, you shouldn't be the only one paying attention to the goals, roles, and rules. *Everyone* should. Members' behavior affects the whole team, not just you. By involving the whole team in monitoring behavior, you foster team ownership of the rules, making it more likely that each person will internalize and follow them.

Yet you may still need to persuade team members to hold one another accountable and give candid feedback, for a few reasons:

- **They avoid the negative.** When people think of accountability, they usually envision calling people out for poor behavior. They don't enjoy bearing bad news, so they try to avoid it. But remind them that giving positive feedback is an equally important part of the equation. Rather than just focusing on what needs fixing, you and other team members will want to acknowledge and reinforce productive behaviors.

- **They're not used to giving feedback.** Growing up, many of us were taught to bounce complaints, injustices, or rule violations up to our parents or teachers or bosses. So we don't have much experience sitting down with a peer and explaining, for example, how that person's late contribution had a negative impact on our own work. We just aren't skilled at it—and we need practice to improve.

- **They don't want to hurt anyone's feelings.** Any feedback conversation has two components: the message you need to deliver and the relationship you want to preserve with the recipient. We often worry that the feedback (particularly if it's peer-to-peer) will harm the relationship. We fear that the recipient will take it personally—that he'll be hurt by the message, angry, suspicious of our intentions, and so on. So it seems easier to keep mum. Instead, you may avoid him, complain about him to others, or become resentful—all of which damages the relationship further. As a result, there's less collaboration and less shared effort, and the work goes downhill.

So how do you get other team members to participate willingly in the monitoring? It can be helpful to lead a frank discussion about feedback itself. Ask how people feel about giving it—and what makes it so hard for them.

Also ask why they think it's worth pushing past that initial difficulty and holding one another accountable. By raising these questions, you'll make everyone's discomfort normal and understandable while signaling that it's something you'll all have to work through together.

You can also frame accountability as a continuous improvement process. That's what we do to refine tasks. It's also what we should do to strengthen relationships. When you see disruptive behaviors and do nothing, you're setting yourself up for frustration: People won't change on their own—they may not even realize they *need* to. Like subpar work, problem behavior will improve only if it's identified and corrected. Enlist your entire team in applauding the good conduct of others (a great motivator and energizer) and in speaking up when unproductive behavior emerges. With that sense of mutual—and ongoing—accountability, the team *will* improve over time, resulting in better outcomes and relationships.

Agreeing on a Process for Accountability

The next step is to sort out how the team will enforce the agreed-upon goals, roles, and rules. (Then in chapter 9, "Hold People Accountable," you'll find exercises to help structure your feedback conversations.) At this point, you'll want to:

Decide how to celebrate successes

Never let a well-done task or accomplishment go by without celebrating it with the team. Plan how you'll recognize achievements and link those rewards to performance metrics and due dates. For example, when the team hits an important milestone, a celebratory dinner out can be a satisfying reward—and an effective motivator.

Schedule periodic continuous improvement meetings

Just as the team monitors its progress toward its goals through regular check-ins, it must also occasionally assess how people are working together (as noted in chapters 3–5). Set aside time for continuous improvement meetings up front, while you're planning the work: When people know that the conversations are coming, they're more inclined to hold *themselves* accountable along the way. Scheduling these meetings also prevents the need for convening a postmortem after things go wrong, which tends to amp up the anxiety.

In the meetings, the team should identify the behaviors and processes that support its goals and those that are getting in the way. Focus on:

- How the *team* is doing as a whole ("Do we need to drop, change, or add any processes or rules in order to work together more effectively?")

- How *individual members* are doing ("What should we continue to do and what should we change?")

Schedule a final debrief

A wrap-up conversation about overall team performance and individual contributions is essential to learning from the experience. (We'll cover this in more detail in chapter 15, "Learn from Your Team's Experiences.")

Again, get this meeting on the calendar up front to make sure that it happens. If you wait until you're nearing the end, you'll find that team members have scattered and you've lost the opportunity to glean lessons and apply them to the next team. This final debrief isn't a remedial intervention; it's just the conclusion of the continuous improvement process you've implemented throughout the team's work together.

Assign the role of goal/rule keeper

As noted in chapter 4, "Agree on Individuals' Roles," it's useful to charge a team member with monitoring compliance and facilitating continuous improvement discussions. This can be one person, or the role can rotate project to project, or even meeting to meeting.

Agree on rules for evaluating work

Determine as a group how you will conduct feedback sessions: Establish, for example, when feedback should be given one-on-one and when it should be offered in a team setting. For example, your team may decide to spend the final five to ten minutes of each meeting discussing "what we did well today" and "what we could have done better." Also set guidelines for how to give and receive feedback.

Building Feedback Skills

Many people have no idea when to give feedback or how to deliver and receive it effectively. As noted earlier, they particularly struggle with negative messages, euphemistically called "constructive feedback" (which we all know means "I don't like what you are doing, and I want you to change"). As a team leader, it's your job to set a good example and provide some training. At the very least, the team should talk about the following principles.

When to give feedback

It's *always* appropriate to give positive feedback, as long as it's specific and genuine—so encourage team members to do it often, both publicly and privately. Negative feedback requires more deliberate timing. Here are some guidelines:

- Provide feedback when someone's behavior prevents you from meeting team goals. *Don't* give it when it's a matter of personal taste and you'd just like to see the other person do things your way.

- Speak up as soon as you can. The longer you wait, the more likely you are either to drop the issue altogether (resolving nothing) or to explode. Those on the receiving end of your pent-up frustration will probably be embarrassed or angry that you've been harboring negative thoughts about them for so long.

- Give negative feedback in a one-on-one conversation whenever possible. Not *all* disruptive behavior merits a group discussion, and you don't want to gang up on individuals—that puts them on the defensive and prevents them from hearing your message. For example, if you had to recheck every number in a teammate's spreadsheet to correct

one on one *first*
then w/ others as needed,
Group = final effort

61

multiple errors, take her aside and ask her to do more checking herself next time before sending the spreadsheet to you.

- Establish rules for when it is appropriate to give negative feedback in a team setting: for instance, when someone's behavior has a negative impact on the entire team or on many members, when the person has already received private feedback but has not demonstrated a willingness to change, or when the feedback is likely to lead to changes in goals, roles, or rules. If you have warring factions inside the team, avoid frustrating "he said, she said" conversations by bringing them together to hear each other's concerns and work out a solution. (More on this in chapter 11, "Resolve Conflicts Constructively.")

How to give feedback

Although the team should follow standard best practices for giving feedback, lead the group in defining its own preferences. They may include principles like these:

- Describe the behavior ("You interrupted me several times"), not the personality ("You were rude").

- Avoid casting behaviors and people as good or bad, right or wrong.

- Don't try to interpret motives behind the behavior; stick with your observations. Say, "You've been late three times," not "It's obvious you aren't committed to this project."

- Point out the behavior's impact on your work. For example: "You waited until after my presentation to say what you didn't like, so I couldn't take your points into consideration before our client meeting."

- Be specific. This is important even for positive feedback. A simple "good job" without details won't show that you've paid attention and really appreciate the work. Give examples, such as "I particularly liked how you answered the customer's questions about our data collection methodology. You avoided jargon and limited your response to exactly what was asked."

- Invite discussion about the problem and alternative solutions.

- Suggest behavior that would be more helpful. In the presentation example above, you might say: "It would be helpful to get your input in advance next time."

- Ask colleagues for permission to give feedback, especially in peer-to-peer situations, where no one has clear authority. For example: "I have some feedback on how you organized your proposal that might make your main idea come through more clearly. Would you like to hear it?" Highlight a benefit (in this case, clarifying the idea) to get your audience to listen.

How to receive feedback

The natural human response to receiving negative stimulus is "fight or flight": We either lash out or withdraw from the situation. It's much more difficult to respond openly and objectively, but that's how people grow and improve. Consider with your team the following ground rules for receiving feedback:

- Control your emotional response. Breathe. If you find it tough to remain calm in the moment, ask for a "time out" to think about the feedback, and resume the conversation later.

- Remember that while all feedback is subjective, it also represents someone else's "reality"—so don't dismiss it if it doesn't align with your perceptions.

- Assume that people giving you feedback have good intentions (that is, that they want to improve how the team works together—they're not out to get you). Resist interpreting their motives. Take their stated reasons at face value.

- Demonstrate that you care about what they're saying. Listen. Request clarification and examples if you're not sure you understand the message.

- Ask people to rephrase their feedback if their delivery doesn't follow agreed-upon team guidelines.

- Ask if they'd like to hear your point of view if you disagree with their feedback. (You might have a different recollection of events, for example.) Someone with good intentions will say yes. Someone who just doesn't like you will say no—or simply not listen.

As with setting rules of conduct, start with a more structured approach to accountability and then ease up. You might, for instance, schedule monthly continuous improvement meetings up front if the team will be working together for a year. Early on you'll want to regularly remind people what the team's goals, roles, and rules are; signal the importance of compliance; and provide some basic training on giving and receiving feedback. You can reduce the frequency or duration of the meetings as team members develop trust and internalize rules. It's easier to cancel unneeded meetings than to add meetings when conflict reaches a crisis level. There's a lot of groundwork to be laid, but once that's done, you switch to maintenance mode.

Finally, you need to consistently hold yourself accountable to meeting the team's goals, respecting its roles, and following its rules. If you don't, you can't credibly hold others accountable for doing the same.

Chapter 7
Commit to a Team Contract

If you've made it this far, you've done a lot of work to build your team's infrastructure. Now it's time to seal the deal.

Nothing secures commitment more than writing up a contract—summarizing what you've agreed to in team-building conversations—and having all members sign it. This solidifies their understanding of what's expected of them, helps in resolving future disagreements, and reminds them of what they've agreed to as you track progress, hold one another accountable, and strive for improvement.

Signing the contract also serves as a symbolic bridge from building the team to working as a team. Consider recognizing the achievement with a dinner out or a toast—a lot of time, energy, and human capital has gone into building a solid foundation for the team.

There's no set format for a team contract, but it's useful to include the following:

- The team's task and process goals

- The team members' roles—how they'll be designated and who will hold them

- Rules of conduct

- How you'll hold one another accountable for producing good work and nurturing strong relationships

See appendix C for a basic template, which you can adapt to suit your team. The contract shouldn't be a lengthy document filled with legalese. Rather, it should be a living document that will evolve and change along with the team.

Once you've got a written and signed agreement, keep it visible to all members as a continual reminder of guiding team principles. You might, for example, display it in a wiki where team members regularly post updates on their tasks. A team of sales reps in a medical devices group made a poster out of its contract, titled the "Declaration of Interdependence," and tacked it up in their conference room. A team at a military manufacturing company summed up its process goals in a slogan ("On time, on place, on target") that members included in their e-mail signatures. If you're leading a long-term or ongoing team, you may even want to put your slogan on coffee mugs so members will have it in front of them all the time.

Rest assured that all this foundational work will pay off: Although teams that jump right into assigning and executing tasks may get a head start on reaching performance goals, research consistently shows that they're soon overtaken by teams that have invested time in establishing their task and process goals, roles, and rules of conduct. Why? Because in all those team-building conversations, members develop trust, the ability to learn from one another, an understanding of how to collaborate fruitfully, and a clear sense of how everyone can best contribute. They then feel more empowered to take on work and solve problems. All of that leads to stronger performance, greater efficiency, and continuous improvement.

Now it's time to focus on the work itself and reap the rewards of your investment.

Section 2
Manage Your Team

Chapter 8
Make Optimal Team Decisions

Much of your team's time together will be devoted to making decisions about the work: planning tasks, monitoring progress, evaluating outcomes, changing strategies, or responding to crises. Teams often struggle with decision making, though. We all have our stories about leaving a meeting confident that everyone knows who's doing what—only to later discover that isn't true. Or getting bogged down in long, tedious discussions about minutiae, losing sight of what's important. Or realizing that hours were spent essentially endorsing a decision the boss had already made.

But you're now well equipped to avoid pitfalls like these. While you were building the team's infrastructure (its goals, roles, and rules), you were also developing the skills a team needs to make good decisions together:

airing dissent, tolerating others' points of view, and making trade-offs, to name a few.

In this chapter, we'll examine best practices for group decision making in the moment.

Think "Good," Not "Right"

We tend to believe deep in our hearts that there's one "right" answer out there, and that it will become evident if we collect enough data and apply enough analytic rigor. Sadly, for most decisions, that's not the case.

Having a discussion about what constitutes an *optimal* decision for the group, versus one that's right, saves everyone the frustration of pursuing unachievable perfection. When your team discussed rules of conduct, members may have agreed on decision-making criteria such as these:

- Take all key factors into account.

- Use the best (often limited) information available.

- Balance data and intuition.

- Rigorously generate multiple options.

- Weigh the pros and cons of each option.

- Get input from everyone who will feel the impact of the decision.

- Support the team's goals.

- Improve the team's ability to solve future problems.

These criteria are not about discovering an end-all, be-all solution. You're just trying to find the best possible answer given whatever constraints the team faces.

Here's an example to show how clear decision-making criteria will expedite that process. A faculty team at a small college found itself at a stalemate after more than a year of debating which core courses all undergraduates must take. Even though all the professors could link their own departments' courses to the school's mission (a critical selection factor), they couldn't agree across departmental lines. But then, after discussing what would constitute a good decision, the team decided that "made in a reasonable period of time" should be a guiding principle. That put everyone in a better frame of mind to meet the fast-approaching deadline for the next year's catalog. The team made compromises on all sides and finalized the curriculum.

Look at the Context

We often associate teams with building consensus. Didn't you pull your team together precisely because you wanted its members' collective brainpower? Yet reaching consensus takes a lot of time and energy—sometimes more than it's worth. Instead of using that as your default approach, consider which type of decision is best for the current situation. Ask yourself:

- **How much time do I have?** If it's in short supply, you may need to make the decision yourself or appoint someone on the team to do it.

- **Who has the expertise?** When one or a few people within the team have greater insight about an issue because of their knowledge or experience, let them make the call—or at least a strong recommendation to the group.

- **Is growth a goal?** If you want members to learn from a decision, spend time discussing it as a group rather than delegating it or making it on your own. Less-experienced members will benefit from hearing subject-matter experts debate which solution is optimal. Members can also develop key skills—such as advocating for a position or challenging someone's point of view—through the decision-making process.

- **How much buy-in do I need?** The greater the commitment you need from team members to implement a decision, the more you'll want to build consensus or at least solicit their input. You'd probably want everyone's buy-in when deciding on the team's strategy for pitching to prospective clients, for example. However, you don't need it to select the PowerPoint template you'll use. Many of those supportive, operational decisions are best delegated to individuals or subgroups.

- **How much creativity does the decision require?** If you're trying to generate really fresh ideas—say you're looking for a new fund-raising concept— don't just sit down at your computer and type up what comes to mind. Ask others to contribute ideas or, better yet, conduct a brainstorming session. Once the team has come up with a long list of possibilities, you'll shift to a different mode of decision making: evaluating and selecting (possibly through the nominal group technique described in chapter 5, "Agree on Rules of Conduct").

Bottom line: Use consensus only when a decision will affect every team member. For big-picture, direction-setting decisions—sorting out or changing rules of conduct, for example—it makes sense. But remember, reaching consensus is not about agreeing on a decision that every member *likes*. You'll drive yourself—and others—mad attempting to arrive at this elusive, usually impossible, destination. Consensus really just means that all members feel they've had a fair hearing so that they'll publicly defend the decision even if it's not in line with their personal preferences.

Majority vote is another option, but use it sparingly. It creates winners and losers—and that division in the group can impede progress, especially if you need people in the minority to implement the decision. People may also interpret your call for a vote as a power play. If it's pretty clear beforehand which side will win, a vote will simply shut down further debate. They know that, and they know you do, too. So save voting for when a deadline looms, when additional delays will damage the team's work, or when the team has already spent too much time trying to reach an agreement. When stalemates occur, it's often because the options are equally good or bad. In that case, vote just to end the gridlock.

Whatever decision-making method you choose, remember to factor in members' need for control and autonomy. Empower people to make decisions connected to their individual roles. If you're delegating a decision to a small group within the team, specify when others can offer input (and when they can't) and have the team agree on what criteria the subgroup should use in making the final decision.

Make It Easy to Contribute

Create an environment where every team member comes to meetings prepared to participate in decision making by advocating, challenging, and proposing alternatives—and by getting behind the group's final choice. You've already set the stage for this by establishing rules for decision making, but people will sometimes need reminders about those rules.

One board chair had several trustees who dominated every decision-making discussion and several who, as a result, rarely bothered to say much. To address that problem, she handed each member five poker chips at a meeting and explained that every time someone spoke, that person had to turn in one chip. Once members used up their chips, they could no longer chime in. The group thought she was joking until she began telling people they'd lost the floor because they'd used up their chips. She made her point, and the team took it to heart. Board members continued to hold one another accountable even without the chips, occasionally saying, "Hey, you've used up your chips. Let's hear from someone else."

Other ways to encourage equal participation include:

- **Acting as a gatekeeper:** Explicitly invite quiet members to speak up. Don't assume that they agree with their teammates or have nothing to add. They may just feel uncomfortable about interrupting to get into the conversation.

- **Resisting the impulse to speed up a decision:** The team may try to quickly narrow down its options or accept the first one on the table just to move things along. But there's value in broadening the field of possibilities before evaluating any of them. Instead of that first or second idea, it may be the ninth or tenth that best meets your needs. You won't get that far if you cut your discussion short.

As team leader, you may feel forced to make a final call, since the team looks to you for guidance. If you want the others to own the decision, push it back on them. Boomerang their "What should we do?" back to them by asking, "What do *you* think we should do?" Or say, "That's up to the group."

That's often a good way to go, because offering your input too soon can quickly shut down a discussion. Once you say, "Wow, that's a great idea—that's what we should do," team members may be reluctant to offer any competing (and possibly better) alternatives. Try waiting until the end of the discussion to offer your ideas or endorse suggestions. When a team member shares an idea that conflicts with your own, watch your body language. You can "kill the messenger" with just one disapproving look.

Of course, when you have expertise that would benefit the discussion, you won't do the team any favors by remaining silent. In a case like that, consider relinquishing your team leader role momentarily so that you're free to participate as a regular member. You might ask an outsider to come in and facilitate. One team leader communicated this role shift by moving out of his usual seat at the head of the table. Another did it by saying, "I'm taking my 'team lead' hat off . . . " before adding her perspectives.

Use Your Experts Wisely

You've included subject-matter experts on your team to provide knowledge, but what if they don't express their insights effectively? Perhaps they give too little input or withhold ideas altogether because they don't want to be held responsible for decisions. You may need to prompt them to share their thoughts so that quality doesn't suffer.

By contrast, when experts give *too much* input, others may see them as condescending and dominating. Or their teammates may abdicate their own responsibility for decisions, thinking, "It's up to the expert." So continually remind all team members of the value they bring: different ideas, new perspectives, ideas not limited to those that worked in the past. Ask them to keep voicing their opinions and to avoid acquiescing too quickly.

Periodically remind the team that each expert's role is to share expertise, not to make decisions unilaterally because of it. You may decide it's best for experts to weigh in later in the discussion if their comments appear to be silencing others early on.

Invite Dissent

Dissent is at the heart of why you've created a team in the first place. Consulting a variety of data sources and examining conflicting ideas will lead to better decisions. If everyone prefers to work with Vendor A, then you won't explore other options, which could include a cheaper supplier with a better track record. If you all agree right away on what the data indicates then you won't conduct further analysis, which might have revealed serious breaches in collection integrity.

Dissent infuses problem solving with energy and creativity. It also promotes closer relationships (as members grow to appreciate one another's contributions), greater social competence (as people learn how to persuade, advocate, and challenge constructively), and psychological well-being (as individuals recognize the value they add in the exchange of ideas).

So why don't teams foster dissent more often? When they're in decision-making mode, the conversation has a task component (evaluating the information) and a people component (maintaining the relationships). Destructive conflict can ensue if dissent starts to feel personal. When someone questions your thinking in a meeting, you might wonder, "Is he trying to make me look bad?" That kind of dissent hurts relationships.

Not surprisingly, many teams attempt to ward off interpersonal conflict by suppressing dissent. We see a team's lack of disagreement as a good thing—but really, it may signal apathy, disengagement, or alienation.

The best teams explore opposing ideas while preserving relationships. But how do you make that happen?

First, agree on what you're trying to accomplish with the decision—perhaps you're looking to woo back a lost client, for example—and then collect as many ideas and views as you reasonably can. Don't finalize big decisions until the group has rigorously examined several options and weighed the pros and cons: This can take the form of a cost/benefit analysis or a discussion of risks and rewards. If the group agrees on one idea quickly, solicit dissent by saying, "Let's see if we can come up with reasons *not* to move forward with this" or "I'd like to hear at least one other proposal before we continue down this path."

You may also provide some time to reflect before making the decision. Ask everyone to think about it until the next meeting. In the interim, talk to people one-on-one. Some members may feel comfortable expressing opposing views in a team setting, but others may not. You may find in these conversations that people start to change their minds—or they may remain aligned. Sometimes early agreement is just that—it's not always a symptom of "groupthink."

Keep the tone constructive. When members state opposing views, have them first paraphrase the other perspective to show that they listened to it and understand it. And protect the dissenters on your team. As they raise concerns, encourage them to say more. As they propose new ideas, ask the team to point out the positives as well as the negatives so people don't simply shoot them down.

Here are several activities for fostering constructive dissent:

Post before you discuss

After you define the problem to solve or the decision to make, have team members post their ideas on a wall (sticky notes work well), and then proceed with a discussion. This brings out views that might otherwise be suppressed once a majority opinion becomes obvious or once the team leader or a major influencer states a position.

Build on written ideas

Have everyone come up with as many ideas as possible, writing each one on a separate piece of paper and placing it in the center of the table. Once members have finished doing this, they can pull out others' papers, read them, jot down why they disagree or how they'd expand the ideas, and put the papers back into the middle. When people stop writing comments, the team reads the ideas out loud and discusses the points others have added to them. You can also do this with flip charts or large sheets of paper tacked on the wall: Members write their ideas on their flip chart and then move around the room to the other charts, reading teammates' ideas and adding comments.

Use advocacy groups

After identifying a few main options, assign each alternative to an advocacy group within the team. Task those groups with developing "best cases" for their assigned options and presenting their positions to the whole team. Once all the groups have presented their cases, they can challenge one another's information, rationales, and conclusions. The outcome is a clearer understanding of the strengths and weaknesses of each position.

Here's an example: In an IT company, an eight-person team was formed to streamline the process of filling customer requests. The team consisted of representatives from two very siloed, embattled functions: customer reps, who took the orders, and technical developers, who completed the orders. The reps proposed a process that made sense to them, but the developers hated it. The developers responded with their own proposal, and the reps hated that. To break the stalemate, the team leader told the reps to strongly advocate for the developers' proposal, and vice versa. This required each side to look at the problem from the other's perspective. As a result, both camps recognized the limitations of their own proposals and the merits of the other side's. They then worked together to create a third proposal that addressed the needs and concerns of both functions.

Play devil's advocate

Early in a discussion, team members may hesitate to actively disagree with one another. Make it safe to do so by assigning the role of devil's advocate to an individual or a subgroup of members. Whenever an idea or position is presented, it's their responsibility to challenge it and identify its weaknesses. This allows people to ask the hard questions or dispute positions without fear of hurting their relationships with their colleagues. It's their *role* to disagree—so others are less likely to take it personally.

To use key decision meetings as learning opportunities, consider ending them with a debrief about the process. You won't do this every time, but it can be useful after a particularly rigorous or contentious debate. Take a few minutes to capture best practices for future decisions, nip bad behaviors in the bud, and review team rules. Try to evaluate the process while it's still fresh. But if people need a little cooling off or reflection time, it's fine to do the debrief at the next meeting or before the next decision. Continuous improvement is your goal.

Chapter 9
Hold People Accountable

When do you start holding the team accountable for its work? Right away.

Don't wait for deadlines to slip—or even for someone to show up 15 minutes late more than once. An accountable team strives for continuous improvement from the outset. There's no time like the present to become more efficient and effective as a group.

Initially, focus your accountability discussions on the team as a whole. Use them to build trust and develop skills in giving and receiving useful feedback. Then you can start having more difficult conversations about individual performance.

Team Accountability

Start small and simple. Do a brief "plus/delta" at the end of every meeting, asking "What did we do well today?

What do we need to change for the next meeting?" Team members might say, for example, that they generated lots of promising ideas but that next time they shouldn't begin analyzing and eliminating options so quickly. You'll want to end the team's conversations about continuous improvement with a plus/delta, too. It may sound circular, but it's the only way your team will get better at giving feedback and holding one another accountable.

These exercises are also useful in assessing team performance.

Discuss what to stop, start, or continue

These three questions are fundamental to any continuous improvement process: "What should we stop? What should we start? What should we continue?" Asking them regularly will build members' feedback skills and trust within the group. A different way of framing this sort of conversation is to ask, "What are some of our greatest achievements so far, and what factors have contributed to those successes? What have been our greatest challenges, and how might we overcome them in the future?"

Rate your team in one area

Ask each member to privately rate the group on some activity or event. It might be as general as "How do you feel about the team's performance on the last project?" or as specific as "How do you feel about the level of support you received from your teammates in the final stretch?" Use a scale of 1 (highly unsatisfied) to 10 (greatly satisfied). When you meet, ask each person to share his or her rating, explain the reason for it, and say what would have to change to increase it.

Even though some team members are inevitably harder "graders" than others, the ratings help people see more clearly what's working for the team and what's not. Saying why they gave the ratings they did will shed light on their own preferences, and saying what needs to change will help the team figure out which rules to fix.

One team leader used this exercise when he noticed tension brewing in his group. No one had complained to him, but people had been uncharacteristically quiet at the past few meetings. He had everyone rate the level of trust among team members. Though several members gave high ratings, two people gave 3s. After they explained their ratings, the problem became clear: In writing a client report together, the two members had divided it into sections that each would prepare. But then one member completely rewrote the other's material when combining the drafted sections into one document. It was a breakdown in roles: One had assumed the editor role, unbeknownst to the other. They agreed that in future joint efforts, they would decide on roles up front.

Rate your team's processes

Want to conduct a more comprehensive review of your team's performance? Try the Process Ratings Exercise (see sidebar). For ongoing teams and long projects, schedule time for this activity quarterly or semiannually; for ad hoc teams or shorter projects, do it at their conclusion.

This exercise measures performance on several key dimensions of teamwork, such as infrastructure, accountability, workload, and trust. However, you can adjust it to meet your needs: Rate only a few elements, for instance. Modify the descriptions at the ends of the scales to include specific behaviors. Or add new scales. If the team consists of people from different parts of the business, you might assess collaboration across functional lines.

Don't buckle under time pressure and skip these conversations because you have 100 tasks that need to be

---

PROCESS RATINGS EXERCISE

Ask members to score the team on the following elements of teamwork, and then meet to discuss. Have them share their ratings, explain their reasoning, and suggest changes that would improve the ratings.

1. Team infrastructure (goals, roles, and rules)

1	2	3	4	5	6	7	8	9	10

Never clearly established; members don't know what's expected of them.

Clearly established; members know what's expected of them.

2. Accountability

1	2	3	4	5	6	7	8	9	10

Members don't comply with team goals and rules; they aren't held accountable.

Members comply with goals and rules; they're held accountable.

3. Workload

1	2	3	4	5	6	7	8	9	10

Team has "free riders" who don't contribute or volunteer; their work gets ignored or is done by a dominant few.

Team has no "free riders"; work is fairly distributed.

4. Problem solving and decision making

1	2	3	4	5	6	7	8	9	10

A few members make all the decisions, with little or no rigor; the team doesn't appreciate opposing ideas.

Team discusses decisions rigorously, seeks diverse ideas, invites dissent, and includes affected stakeholders.

5. Managing conflict

1	2	3	4	5	6	7	8	9	10

Members avoid conflict or pretend it doesn't exist; people complain about others behind their backs.

Members explicitly discuss conflicts with all those involved.

6. Task/project progression

1	2	3	4	5	6	7	8	9	10

Members do poor-quality work and miss deadlines.

Members produce high-quality work on time.

7. Communication

1	2	3	4	5	6	7	8	9	10

Members don't communicate; they fail to disclose decisions, rationales, goals, and other information critical to performance.

Members communicate frequently and fluidly; they fully disclose decisions, rationales, goals, and other information critical to performance.

8. Trust

1	2	3	4	5	6	7	8	9	10

Members don't trust one another, which stifles innovation, risk taking, and rigorous decision making; they expect their input to be misinterpreted or leaked to people outside the team.

Members have a high degree of trust, which fosters innovation, risk taking, and rigorous decision making; they expect their input to be received openly and kept confidential.

done. It's tempting to do so, even when things are going well on a team. But resist that urge. It's as important to acknowledge what's going well, so people continue that behavior, as it is to identify and fix what's broken.

As with any continuous improvement discussion, have someone record the group's observations and resulting decisions. This record will help you update the team's roles and rules as they evolve.

Individual Accountability

As members gain experience in holding the team accountable, it's time to add in discussions that focus on individuals. To help people with that transition, allow them time to carefully prepare their remarks in advance. You'll also want to review the team's rules about how to give and receive feedback (see chapter 6, "Set the Stage for Accountability") and remind people that the overarching goal of the discussion is to continuously improve individual performance for the benefit of the team. Members should always use that lens when deciding what to share in a feedback session.

To keep discussions focused and constructive, you can modify the team exercises described earlier in this chapter. Familiarity with those structured conversations may help members overcome their natural reluctance to give their peers feedback.

The stop-start-continue exercise works particularly well for individuals. Approach it the same way you would a team-focused discussion: Ask everyone to consider each member: "What do you want this person to stop doing? What do you want him to start doing? What do you want him to continue doing?" Have people write down their comments in advance and then meet to share their thoughts. Remind them to describe specific behaviors, not personalities, so their observations don't come across as personal attacks.

Remember the community health care team that Nancy, the nurse, drove crazy with all her questions (chapter 2, "Get to Know One Another")? To avoid future misunderstandings about one another's intentions, members began conducting stop-start-continue discussions on a quarterly basis. Over time, they dubbed these "Kudos and Concerns" meetings, where members could give each person an unlimited number of kudos (for behaviors to continue) and point out two areas of concern (behaviors to manage).

It's essential to limit the number of behaviors to manage. Realistically, most people can work on one or two areas at a time. They may feel overwhelmed by more than that.

After each member receives feedback, call out themes and ask individuals what behaviors they'll commit to stopping, starting, or continuing. You may need to give them time to think about this first, as it involves digesting and accepting what they've heard. Allowing them to decide what they'll do empowers them. Feedback is subjective, after all, and members may have conflicting responses to behaviors (for instance, one may appreciate someone's close attention to detail, and another may find it frustrating).

Group feedback is powerful because we all feel a basic need for affiliation. Team discussions harness the power of the group and compel individuals to get with the program—it's like high-school peer pressure channeled for the good. This approach (versus a one-on-one conversation) is most useful when:

- **The behavior affects the whole team's ability to perform.** Talking with the group enables people to see the broader impact of their actions. Completing tasks late doesn't just hurt the person waiting for them—it hurts the full team. That realization usually prompts members to comply with the team's expectations.

- **The behavior is best handled by adjusting the team's expectations.** Take Isaac, a financial analyst on a client support team who was continually late for the group's daily 9:00 a.m. check-in meeting. Through the stop-start-continue exercise, team members told Isaac he needed to change this behavior. He then revealed that he was responsible for dropping off his son at day care, and even when he arrived there at the earliest possible drop-off time, the public transportation schedule didn't permit him to get to work by 9:00. With that information, the team changed the meeting time to 9:30.

Despite the power of accountability, some individuals may choose to not do the work or comply with agreed-upon rules. It's your job as team leader to manage individual performance. After you've let problem members know that they aren't doing what's expected of them, here are some other steps you can take:

- **Confirm that they have the skills to do what your team needs.** Can they demonstrate those skills? Have they used those skills in other situations? If not, you will need to train and coach them or work more closely with them to build the required competencies. Although you may enlist team members to assist in their skill development—for example, by partnering up on tasks—the coaching responsibility primarily falls to you. As people are getting up to speed, give them smaller tasks, shorter timelines, more observation, and more feedback.

- **Make sure they have the resources to do the work and follow team rules.** Isaac, in the earlier example, couldn't get to team meetings on time because of child care and transportation constraints, so his team changed the meeting time. Consider how you can provide missing resources for your team members or help them overcome obstacles to performance.

- **Zero in on what motivates them.** If your team members know that they're not meeting expectations, they possess the skills and resources to do the work, and you don't see any other barriers impeding their performance, then they are probably lacking motivation. Again, as the team leader, it's up to you to identify whether they respond best to

recognition, control, achievement, or affiliation—
all big motivators. The first three can be tricky to
satisfy in a team setting: Recognition for group
accomplishments must be shared. So must control.
And depending on others to produce results can
dampen an individual's sense of achievement. You
may have more luck appealing to each member's
need to belong to the group. But keep in mind
that lack of motivation is often a reason to cut
someone loose.

Ideally, you'll have the authority to remove nonproductive or disruptive members from your team. If that is
not automatically granted, negotiate for it. Without this
authority, you may get stuck with people who don't carry
their weight, which can have a demoralizing effect on the
rest of the team.

The IT team leader who used advocacy groups (from
chapter 8, "Make Optimal Team Decisions") faced that
problem. After multiple accountability conversations,
one technical developer kept reverting to the old siloed
way of filling customer requests instead of following the
new protocols the team had agreed on. His recalcitrance
led to unhappy customers and frustrated colleagues.
Unfortunately, the team leader didn't have the authority to remove anyone from the group. So he isolated the
offending member, protecting the rest of the team from
the disruptive behavior. The engineer followed his own
protocol: Instead of collaborating with the team to fill
requests, he worked alone. The team leader held him
accountable only for his own outcomes, and he did not

participate in any team meetings. The developer pulled his weight but was essentially an individual contributor.

Although this may seem like an inequitable or easy-way-out solution, it's sometimes the best one for the team, the individual, and even you (fewer headaches!). You need to decide how much time and energy you want to invest in fixing the behaviors or outcomes of a problem member. If you've chosen that person for his content expertise, you might treat him like a consultant, pulling him in as needed without involving him in ongoing team building and maintenance.

Accountability conversations are important throughout the life of the team. Here, we've discussed how to continuously improve by aligning behavior with the team's aspirations (embedded in its rules). In the next chapter, we'll turn to another aspect: giving team members recognition for their good work. And chapter 15 covers the final step of accountability: reviewing each individual's contributions to identify which behaviors and processes to bring to future teams and which to change. This enables you to learn from each team experience and build your own competence as a team leader over time.

Chapter 10
Give People Recognition

Even in team environments, recognition remains one of the top four human motivators (along with the need for achievement, control, and a sense of belonging).

It's relatively easy to recognize the full team for good task work, such as meeting goals and hitting deadlines, or for exemplary behavior, such as conducting a difficult feedback session constructively. It can be harder, in a team setting, to recognize *individuals* for their good work or behaviors. Teams are based on collaboration, equity, and fairness. How can you give individuals their due while fostering the cohesiveness that comes when everyone works toward the same goals and follows the same rules?

The Japanese proverb, "The nail that sticks up gets hammered down," comes to mind. Sadly, that's what often happens to individuals who get a lot of praise from their team leader: Other team members may begin competing for your attention or, worse, sabotaging the work of your "pets."

You need to give recognition to motivate individuals—and certain team members do regularly go the extra mile. Here are some tips.

Connect One-to-One

You can do lots of things to discreetly show your appreciation for individuals' contributions. For starters, get to know each member personally. Find out about people's backgrounds, lives outside work, and interests. For example, does a team member bike for a cancer charity? If so, ask about her latest race and consider donating to the cause.

Learn about people's career aspirations, too, and pass along relevant articles, blog posts, or other information you come across. Introduce team members to people in your network who can help advance their careers. You might even sponsor them in professional development training or write letters of recommendation for school or fellowship applications.

You can also privately provide extra feedback, going beyond the performance appraisals the team conducts. One of the most powerful forms of recognition is to help people grow. Assign them challenging tasks, and coach them. Pass on positive comments you've heard about them from others. And give them as much time and attention as you reasonably can.

Written acknowledgments go a long way, too. Send a note of thanks, for example, and copy senior management and HR.

Include Positive Feedback

Make sure the team gives positive feedback in its accountability discussions (chapter 9, "Hold People Accountable"). Don't just focus on behaviors that should be added, dropped, or changed. Give recognition during discussions about behaviors that people should continue, and occasionally conduct a session devoted just to sharing positive feedback. Go around the room, and ask everyone to say what they appreciate about each team member. Try prompting people to comment on specific contributions (to a particular task or project) as well as general strengths (skills, attitude, and so on).

A design team at an engineering company conducted a positive feedback session immediately following a big team failure: The prototype it had produced came back from the engineering group with a long list of attributes deemed infeasible. While the team pondered everything that had contributed to this failure, its leader wanted to boost morale by reminding people of the talents and strengths they brought to the new challenge. The appreciation exercise helped the team members see that they had the skills and smarts to come up with a successful new design.

Share Credit Publicly

Visibility outside the group is another effective form of recognition. Consider having every member sign the proposals and project reports submitted by the team. Or ask every member to participate in final presentations to clients or senior management.

A senior scientist in a pharmaceutical laboratory saw a dramatic increase in individuals' motivation (and, consequently, their contributions) when she changed how the lab gave credit to employees. She didn't like the fact that only her name would appear on research reports and academic articles in medical journals. This made the rest of the team's work invisible to the outside world. Over time, it became increasingly difficult to get junior scientists and research analysts to put in the extra time and energy needed to meet project deadlines. So she changed the lab's practice, giving recognition to junior scientists and research analysts. When team members could claim authorship on reports and articles, their motivation soared. The lab began meeting its deadlines and found itself deluged with applications for junior positions.

Think about your interactions with team members as bank transactions: Every time you give constructive feedback or hold someone accountable, you're withdrawing on your account. Every time you give positive feedback or recognition, you're making a deposit. Clearly, you always want to be "in the black." This means making timely, consistent deposits. You'll get a great return on your investment.

Chapter 11
Resolve Conflicts Constructively

Most of us go to great lengths to avoid conflicts. We smile and nod instead of proposing alternatives. We give in and do things "their way." We'll deny outright that conflicts even exist when asked (the "Nothing's wrong—everything's great" scenario). But on teams, conflicts are inevitable.

Why Conflicts Arise

Typically, team members don't try to cause trouble or seek negative attention. More often, they become embroiled in conflicts for several reasons:

- **Different work styles.** To arrive at a team contract, members had to compromise. Most likely, at least a few rules of conduct don't jibe with their own personal preferences. That's why team-building conversations can be so difficult: It's not easy for people to change their ways. It's even harder when the stakes are high. After all, a team's output can affect individuals' salaries, careers, and reputations. Before signing the contract, people may have resisted certain rules—not out of petulance but from a desire to do what's worked for them in the past.

You've done a lot of work to preempt style-based conflicts, yet they'll still flare up now and then, particularly when deadlines loom, people get overworked, or the team experiences a setback. When we're tired or stressed, we all tend to revert to the way we act most naturally, with no mental pause, no behavioral adjustment. For example, under time pressure, a team member might make a decision unilaterally, despite what the team had agreed.

- **Opposing ideas, perspectives, and opinions.** As we discussed earlier, the diversity you carefully built into your team often leads to disagreements. If your team is operating as it should, people will voice dissenting opinions—and that's a healthy kind of conflict. Your team's rules of conduct will help keep tempers in check, warding off feelings of being dismissed or "spoken down to." When people give in to those feelings, however, teams experience the third source of conflict.

- **Anger or hurt feelings.** This is what most people think of when they hear the word *conflict:* One member mad at another. One person offended by someone's comments. Subgroups vying to "win" a decision. Individuals taking outcomes personally. We've all been on teams that feel like a war zone.

How do *you* react in situations like these? Do you lash out, raising your voice and slinging a few choice words? Or do you try to bargain your way out of the conflict, suggesting that you and your opponent "split the difference" or "agree to disagree"? If you're like many people, you won't directly confront the colleague who offended you (although you might talk to *others* about the problem). You delay answering her calls and avoid eye contact at meetings.

We often avoid dealing with interpersonal conflict because we don't know how to handle it or because we had disastrous experiences in the past. We withdraw and hope it goes away on its own.

The individuals seated around your table may respond in any of those ways. But that's exactly why you spent time creating rules for dealing with conflict back in your team-building conversations (see chapter 5, "Agree on Rules of Conduct").

Before you even start talking about the problem, first review those rules with the team. For instance, you all may have agreed to acknowledge the ways in which you've each contributed to the problem. You also may have decided to discuss conflicts openly with the people involved, to resist the impulse to counterattack, and to control emotional responses (no profanity, threats, or stalking out of the room).

Taking the time to review the rules you established when you were not actually *in* conflict will allow you to have a more productive conversation, and perhaps even to act in accordance with the ideal behaviors you laid out when it was all hypothetical.

How to Handle Conflicts

Yelling or giving in won't fix anything. Nor will splitting the difference, which often compromises quality or results in an outcome no one likes. How, then, can you pave the way to resolution?

Identify the cause

Instead of viewing conflict as something to avoid, look at it as a red flag: Something is breaking down, but what is it? Just as you'd investigate why a product line didn't perform up to expectations or why a marketing launch didn't yield the targeted response rate, you need to understand *why* the conflict has arisen. Ask those involved what they are hoping to achieve. Their answers may reveal opposing intentions—for instance, one person wants to finish a project quickly, while the other wants to do it perfectly.

Opposing intentions may mean that individuals are operating with different goals in mind—often the most fundamental reason for conflict. Even though you worked together up front to formulate *team* goals, over time people's interpretations may have splintered into different directions. Certain goals may no longer be salient, or new ones may need to be added. Reconfirming *why* you're working together and what you're all trying to accomplish helps get everyone back on the same page.

If you've reviewed your goals together and yet there's still a problem, you'll need to dig deeper. Try asking the same questions you'd use to uncover a task breakdown:

- What's working?

- What's not working?

- When did it stop working? What in the environment changed at the time of the shift—team membership? The task? Other events?

- Who is part of the conflict? Who isn't? Why?

- Who has the upper hand, and in what way? Who is "losing," and in what way? (Answers to both these questions can uncover resistance to resolving the conflict.)

You can also explore what's going on *around* the conflict:

- What driving forces are exacerbating the problem? (A client's increasing dissatisfaction? A competitive threat in the marketplace? Factors like these can ratchet up the urgency.)

- What's preventing the situation from getting better? (Competing demands on time? Understaffing? You'll need to address these to resolve the conflict.)

Revisit the team's rules

Most people operate with good intentions, believing that they're contributing to the team's goals and behaving in accordance with team norms. Conflict can still creep in, however, because it's impossible to outline expectations for every scenario you'll encounter. What's more, people often assign different meanings to the same words. Conflict is a good opportunity to investigate and repair whether you need to create new rules, clarify existing ones, or pull individuals back into alignment.

For example, your team may be ready to strangle one member who keeps repeating his idea over and over again as the team tries to reach agreement. His behavior, which other team members find rigid and overbearing, means it takes forever to make a decision. Increasingly, they just "give up" and let his ideas prevail. Revisiting the team's rules as a group will allow members to take such behavior into account, focusing on:

- **Gaps we may not have noticed when articulating our rules.** Did we anticipate all the challenges we might encounter? Now that we've lived as a team for a while, do we need to create new rules?

- **Whether our existing rules are explicit and effective.** Is the language clear enough? For example, when the team created the rule "Advocate your position well in team decisions" our goal was to encourage rigorous exploration of lots of good options. But in practice, "advocate" means different things to different people (relentless hounding, in this case). Conflict can arise from even well-intentioned behavior (for example, we thought having a devil's advocate during decision making would be useful, but perhaps we need to scale it back to having someone play that role only for certain types of decisions).

- **Whether individuals have "drifted" from the rules.** Even if everyone was in lock-step with the rules in the beginning, over time, people's recollections and interpretations may have shifted. Our memories often fail us when we're under stress or we may revert to our own preferred behavior in a crisis.

One way to expose the differences in people's expectations or interpretations is to ask team members to write down what they believe the team's goals and rules are. Then, review the responses as a group, and note how consistent their answers are. Go over the team contract together and ask the group, "Are these goals and rules still valid? Should we change them? What's missing?" If most people aren't following what's documented, make tweaks to reflect actual practice.

Point out strengths

In times of conflict, it's easy to demonize others. *They're* the ones who yelled. *They're* the ones who caused a bottleneck. And so on. During all the finger-pointing, people forget about the value everyone brings to the team. So bring the strengths and skills of others to their attention before talking about the conflict. These next two structured conversations can help cut through the tension, remind people that they're complementary teammates (not adversaries), and preempt defensiveness.

Even if you've already used the Artifact Exercise to highlight individuals' strengths back when you introduced your team members (see chapter 2, "Get to Know One Another"), try it again. Ask each person to share an accomplishment external to the team. This allows members to see everyone in a positive light and get a fuller picture of one another, beyond the work they do together.

The power of this next exercise comes from having others sing each member's praises. Have the team sit in a circle around a table. Ask one person at a time to turn her back to the group while the rest of you talk about her strengths, what she brings to the team, and how she contributes. She's not allowed to say a word in response. Speak loudly enough for her to hear all the good things you're saying. Spend about two minutes per person.

Foster empathy

Empathy is a critical ingredient in conflict resolution. Do what you can to promote it. For instance, you might ask individuals or small subgroups with different perspectives to prepare three-minute skits acting out, on fast-forward, a day in their hectic lives. This gives them all a chance to highlight—in an entertaining way—some of the daily challenges they face. Encourage them to exaggerate, both to punch up the humor and to drive their points home. This exercise helps everyone recognize that seemingly combative behaviors, such as curt language or omitting colleagues from an e-mail thread, are often attempts to deal with time pressure, reconcile competing demands, and so on. With that empathic view, people are less likely to assume malicious intent and may lower their defenses.

The sales and fulfillment groups at a consumer products distribution company used this exercise to address a classic conflict: Fulfillment folks felt that sales reps made ridiculous promises to customers, and they resented having to "move heaven and earth" to deliver on those contracts. They complained about frequent rush orders and exceptions to shipping protocols. Sales reps viewed the people in fulfillment as inflexible and totally out of touch with the realities of the marketplace.

After a little prodding, each group created a "day in the life" skit. These skits featured every imaginable disruption, setback, screw-up, and bad-news event. Both groups came away with a clearer sense of their colleagues' challenges and pressures. They then worked together to redesign their fulfillment processes. Sales reps had previously tagged most customer requests as "special" or "rush"; after seeing what fulfillment had to deal with as a result, sales put a cap on those, making them exceptions rather than the norm. And fulfillment redistributed routine tasks to free up staff time and capacity to satisfy special requests when they came through.

Reframe the conflict

By phrasing the conflict in constructive language and focusing on solutions, you'll depersonalize the problem. If one member consistently fails to finish tasks on time, the group does need to hold her accountable, but avoid defining it this way: "Maura always turns her work in late." Instead, ask each member to state the problem in a solution-oriented way: "how to create processes that enable Maura to complete her work on time." That gets people thinking about the future instead of wallowing in

TRUTHS ABOUT CONFLICT

Consulting with teams and leading my own, I've experienced the following truths about conflict again and again. Once you absorb them, have a discussion with your team early on, preferably *before* any problems crop up.

Unnamed conflicts remain unresolved. Conflicts do not go away on their own. Rather, they intensify as work pressures mount. So discuss them as soon as possible. Task-oriented team members tend to believe they can "just push through this," hoping to complete their work and meet their deadlines. They often feel they don't have time to talk about conflicts. People-oriented members worry that discussion will lead to hurt feelings and severed relationships. And members of ad hoc teams may think, "I have to work with this group for only three more weeks, so why bother talking about this? I can put up with anything for that long." However, avoidance leads to the next problem.

Ignored conflicts hurt the team's work. People focus less on their tasks if they're wasting time and energy avoiding one another, and quality suffers as a result. Withdrawal from the group amounts to lost the past. If Maura doesn't have to sit through rehashing of her continual lateness, she's less likely to be defensive—and more likely to engage in the conversation and change her behavior. Plus, having every team member state the problem brings out different perspectives. For

resources (brainpower, sets of hands). As members stop talking to one another, they may duplicate work or find at the end of a project, when writing up the final report, that their work isn't cohesive. For all these reasons, members must get problems out in the open.

You can't resolve every conflict. This is hard for team leaders to accept: Unless all affected parties want to resolve a conflict, they won't. So what should you do if someone deliberately perpetuates the conflict—drawing it out as a way of holding a decision hostage, for example? What if he passive-aggressively signals his unhappiness by sabotaging tasks—skipping important steps or not verifying data? Refusal to resolve conflict is a violation of basic team rules. If someone refuses to discuss an issue, or nothing changes after you've talked, you might need to isolate that member from the others (as discussed in chapter 9, "Hold People Accountable") so that their behaviors don't bring the work to a halt or threaten its quality. Or, if you have the authority, remove that person from the team.

example, one member may see the problem as "how to get the project done on time"; another may see it as "how to develop people's skills so they can get their portions done on time"; still another may see it as "how to prioritize all the challenges each member faces." To craft a viable solution, everyone needs to be solving the same problem.

As discussed earlier, it's equally important to look at what *is* working. In Maura's case, the team could talk about times when she did get her work in on deadline. This acknowledges the good work Maura does, and it may somewhat reduce her need to defend herself. (Rarely is a member *always* late or *always* creating problems.) It also provides the team with data for coming up with a solution: What variables allowed her to meet her deadlines? Did a different person do the delegating? How did the tasks differ? Were they less complex? More squarely in her comfort zone? Did she have more time? Did the work require fewer interactions with others? Identifying contextual differences often reveals a solution.

Envision the future

The more you gear your conversations toward the future, the more productive they will be. Rigorously deconstructing the events that led up to a conflict, even with the best intentions of understanding the causes, can still put people in a blaming frame of mind.

Once again, think continuous improvement. Ask the team, "What do we need to do differently going forward?" For instance, what reporting relationships need to change? What timelines? What team processes? How can you or others change the context to prevent unhelpful behavior in the future?

Teams in conflict often feel consumed by how terrible and overwhelming their current situation is. Try to get people to lift their heads up from the present and look toward where they want to go. Ask them to describe how they'd *like* the team to operate, what kinds of relationships they *want* with their teammates, what caliber of work they'd *like* to produce. You've had this conversation before (see chapter 3, "Establish Your Team's Goals"); but you'll want to revisit these issues now and then, and a conflict is a good opportunity to do so. The next exercise is one way of doing this.

Ask each member to prepare a "farewell letter" to the team. Have people reflect on what they'd be most proud of about the team's work and, more important, the way members worked together. At the meeting, invite individuals to share their letters, and then discuss what was important to each person. Often themes will emerge across letters, revealing the source of the conflict and what needs to change.

That's what happened when an alumni board at a small college did this exercise. Over the years, the group had served largely as a mouthpiece for its president and the college deans. As new people joined, they became increasingly frustrated with the board's passive, complacent culture. To root out the conflict between new and legacy members, each person wrote a farewell letter answering the question "In what position do you want the school to be in when you leave?" They used that as a starting point for crafting a unified vision and, from there, agreed on which actions the team would take to push for that vision.

The goals and rules you've already established will guide your team in resolving conflicts. But as you can see, those conflicts will serve to refine the goals and rules to prevent problems down the road (see the sidebar "Truths About Conflict"). Once again, it's a process of continuous learning and improvement.

Chapter 12
Welcome New Members

When your team gains or loses even one member, its composition changes. It becomes a new team, with a different mix of skills and temperaments, so you'll need to review (and possibly redefine) goals, roles, and rules. If you don't, here's the kind of problem you might encounter:

As VP of market development at a fairly young health care start-up, Steve had built a tight team of eight account reps, each in charge of a different region of the New England area. After three years, the team lost one of its reps and brought in Carol as a replacement. Carol quickly learned the business, but she had trouble integrating with her new team. Other members complained about her to Steve: They said she was taking over client relationships without permission, writing "sharp" e-mails, and challenging them in embarrassing ways. They thought she was aggressive, disrespectful, and inconsiderate. How, they wondered, had they misjudged her so badly when interviewing her for the job?

Maybe Carol had pulled the wool over their eyes during the hiring process and was really a ruthless, competitive colleague who didn't care about people. But more likely, she hadn't been brought up to speed on the team's expectations. Had anyone told her that before taking on a client relationship she needed to speak to the rep in charge of that region? Or that the team valued its collaborative culture? Or that if she disagreed with someone, she needed to discuss it privately? Probably not, Steve realized.

Ideally, a team's veteran members will orient the new ones, filling them in on the rules. Even better, the whole (new) team will discuss whether the old ways of working still apply and what may need to change. Unfortunately, that's not what usually happens. When adding someone new, teams tend to explain what the tasks are but gloss over how the group prefers to interact. They expect their new teammate to pick up that information along the way, or they point out rules after she violates them ("Yeah, not a good idea to just pop into his office with a question— you really need an appointment").

Given the time you've already spent on team building, you might not relish the thought of revisiting the process. You may be thinking, "We've done all that! We've got work to do!" But think of the rewards you'll reap: a fully invested, integrated new member and a more cohesive, productive team.

As you're taking a fresh look at your team's infrastructure, you'll want to:

- **Recognize the impact of any departures.** Before
new people come on board, acknowledge how the
team has changed as a result of losing a member.
At this point, you're not just wondering who's going
to become the resident software expert. That's only
the "task" side of the loss. You'll certainly need to
deal with it—missing competencies should guide
who you hire or how you redistribute responsibilities among remaining team members. But there's
also a "people" side: Legacy members may feel sad,
abandoned, envious, or even relieved when a teammate leaves. It's critical to give them a chance to
air their emotional responses, whether it's through
a good-bye lunch or a conversation about how
they're feeling. It allows the team to clear the air
of past issues, identify important changes to make,
and refocus members on their work.

- **Celebrate the addition of new members.** If you're
hiring new employees, of course you'll do all the
regular onboarding: setting up their new work
spaces, training them, explaining their responsibilities, familiarizing them with company poli-
cies, and so on. But again, those are task-related
activities. What can you do on the "people" side to
help new members? As the team leader, how can
you address their anxiety, excitement, or feelings
of separateness?

  Throughout the centuries, groups have per-
formed ceremonies to receive new members into
adulthood, religious sects, the military, fraternities,

and gangs. Though you probably won't give your new members tattoos or have them fast for a week, the basic idea is the same: Accept them into the group with some sort of celebration or initiation rite. You might host a dinner at your house, for example. One team leader situated newcomers in the office next to his. The close proximity allowed for frequent informal check-ins and ensured that lots of foot traffic passed by the new person's desk.

- **Make meaningful introductions.** Legacy members already know about everyone's skills, interests, and idiosyncrasies. But you need to share all that information with your new members—it will help them bond and interact with the group. This can be fun. Try having veterans introduce one another to their new teammates by going around the room and completing the following sentence: "What you should know about Ava is . . . ." Or you might ask people to describe the funniest (or worst or most embarrassing) thing that's happened to them since they've joined the team. It doesn't really matter how you frame the exercise, as long as it gives new members a sense of what individuals are like.

- **Highlight personalities and work styles.** The goal here is to reveal how each person works in a team setting, as you did in chapter 2, "Get to Know One Another." If continuing members completed a personality diagnostic such as Myers-Briggs, have new ones do it, too. Then invite all members to share their results. You may even want legacy folks to comment on one another's traits, describing how they've seen those tendencies play out ("I could see that Debbie was an ESFP type when she . . . "). Or have people talk about their own work styles, completing sentences such as "When I make decisions, my biggest concern is . . . " and "When I'm under pressure, I tend to . . . ."

- **Adjust your team's process.** Although you want new people to learn about the team's established ways of working together, you also want veterans to learn about the new members' preferences. That way, the team can renegotiate an infrastructure that reflects everybody. Revisit the exercises you've done to define goals, roles, and rules (see chapters 3–5), and by all means, share the team contract with the new person. But make sure that legacy members comment on how things work in practice—and then update the goals, roles, and rules accordingly. And ask new members to talk about their experiences on past teams: what worked well, what didn't, and what lessons might apply in this new context.

Integrating new members in a deliberate way enables them to contribute more quickly and the team to adjust to its new future together. You've already invested lots of time in recruiting the right members, old and new. It's worth investing a little more in keeping the group humming.

Chapter 13
Manage Outside the Team

You've already done a lot of work to organize, motivate, and manage your team. But to meet your goals, it's equally important to motivate and manage people *outside* your team, up and down the hierarchy.

MIT management professor Deborah Ancona calls this *boundary management:* You cultivate mutually beneficial relationships with colleagues elsewhere in the organization—particularly the people your team relies on for information and resources. If you don't manage boundaries, team performance suffers.

Consider this cautionary tale: A branch manager at a regional bank had high aspirations (task goals) for innovative customer service, so he worked with his team of 10 employees to define them and put them into practice. Though customers liked the changes they saw, internal relationships across the organization became strained.

The corporate compliance department grew frustrated as branch employees continually asked for exceptions to existing rules. Corporate marketing resisted the branch's requests for variations to branding protocols. And other branch managers resented this branch for getting "special treatment." Within a year, it had a reputation as a problem child, not as an innovator. Eventually the executive team replaced the branch manager.

If the manager had thought about the impact his team's innovations would have on others in the organization, he could have partnered with them instead of alienating them. For example, he might have included them in brainstorming sessions or solicited their input before changes came their way.

So consider your team's work from the perspective of your stakeholders—the individuals and groups who will have the greatest impact on your team's success. They may include:

- senior managers who control your resources

- leaders of other teams competing for company resources

- managers of groups whose collaboration or input your team needs

- managers who have "loaned" people to your team on an ad hoc basis

- functional groups (marketing, engineering, accounting) who provide support

To identify your stakeholders and map out your relationships with them, draw an X on a whiteboard and say, "This is us." Next draw incoming arrows labeled with all the resources you need (and who owns them) and outgoing arrows labeled with all the people and groups who will use what you're producing. Your project plans also reveal the interconnected relationships your work entails.

Once you've identified which parties will require care and feeding, manage your team's boundaries by establishing a reputation, providing external value, and assigning boundary roles. Let's look at each of those steps in more detail.

Establish a Reputation

To obtain the people, funding, commitment to timing, and cross-functional collaboration your team requires, you must earn a favorable reputation early on with decision makers in the senior ranks. As Deborah Ancona's research shows, their first impression of your team will stick—and it will significantly influence your team's success or failure. If your stakeholders like what they see, they'll spread the word, and others in the organization will eagerly help you out. Everyone likes backing a winner.

For a brief period after you've assembled your team, you've got a clean slate: Senior managers haven't formed an opinion about you either way. That's your chance to forge a positive impression.

Suppose you're submitting your team's first progress report, for instance, or releasing a beta version of your software program. From this early glimpse of your team's work, top management will form its opinion, which will then spread rapidly through the organization.

Initial communication matters a lot. If it reveals any kind of struggle within your team—difficulty meeting a deadline or a goal, for example—you'll have to fight the uphill battle from then on of overcoming a bad reputation. Senior managers may question your team's competence, reconsider whether the work you're doing is even necessary, or signal in some way their withdrawal of confidence or support. Others inside the organization will follow suit, thinking why get behind a losing team? Additionally, people will view your subsequent efforts through that lens of negativity, emphasizing missteps and even attributing any success to luck instead of competence. Expectations of failure will become a self-fulfilling prophecy.

How do you manage your reputation to prevent that from happening? By controlling information flow. Discuss up front with your team who should communicate with whom, and what information to share. At one small nonprofit, the executive committee actually used the last part of every team meeting to craft external talking points so that they'd all be on the same page once they'd left the conference room.

Carefully consider who will be the "face" of your team. Send only the most positive, articulate, and politically savvy team members to meet with senior managers, deliver status updates, and so on.

Also, embed small, early wins in your project plan—important outcomes the team can quickly and easily accomplish. Delivering right away on these promises shows that the team is competent, well organized, and primed for success. Even if you then miss a deadline later on, the senior team will probably see it as a temporary setback. Identifying early wins often involves breaking a larger task into smaller pieces. One team at a nonprofit, which focused on giving children access to science education, was charged with getting six new corporations to fund community outreach programs. Instead of waiting to achieve all six goals, the team widely publicized its first success—and then its second. Word quickly spread that the team was on a roll.

Provide External Value

As a team leader, you can't require that people in other groups support you. You have to make them *want* to. You can win them over by invoking what Allan Cohen and David Bradford call "the law of reciprocity" in their book *Influence Without Authority*. It's the "almost universal belief that people should be paid back for what they do." When colleagues do something for you, they expect you to help them at some point—and when you do something for them, they feel obliged to reciprocate.

Once you've identified the people and groups you need to rely on to meet your goals, figure out what you can do for them. Consider how you might support them in achieving their own goals. They may respond well, as Cohen and Bradford suggest, to an exchange "of tangible goods, such as a budget increase, new equipment, or more personnel; of tangible services, such as a faster response time, more information, or public support; or of sentiments, such as gratitude, admiration, or praise."

Determine which "currencies" they value, and start paying. You can earn reciprocity points with your finance colleagues simply by submitting your budget proposal on time and in good shape. Timeliness, accuracy, and attention to detail are all valuable to them. And they'll be more inclined to reciprocate when you ask for help on a task that calls for number crunching, such as building a business case.

You'll gain influence with people only when you're "in the black"—when you've done more for them than they've done for you. That's not to say you should keep a running tally of favors exchanged. But make an ongoing effort to be helpful. Don't wait until you need something to do something for them.

Assign Boundary Roles

To manage your team's boundaries properly, it's helpful to understand the roles Deborah Ancona outlines for controlling the flow of information. Their overall purpose is to make sure outgoing messages enhance the team's reputation and incoming messages enable the group to do its best work.

Managing two-way flow

The "task coordinator" occupies the role we most typically associate with boundary management. This is the person who gathers external approvals to proceed with tasks, negotiates for resources, coordinates the team's activities with other people's schedules, and solicits external feedback. The task coordinator both shares and receives information across the team's boundaries.

Managing outward flow

The "ambassador" focuses on team PR. This person establishes relationships with key stakeholders, updates them on progress, and strategically shares information to influence perceptions and generate support. The "guard," conversely, ensures that confidential information remains inside the team, often creating and enforcing protocols for data storage and dissemination.

Managing inward flow

The "scout" actively seeks external information so that the team avoids surprises and can capitalize on opportunities. This person scans the environment for trends in markets, technology, competitive products, and ideas, and identifies potential allies and opponents. The "sentry," on the other hand, monitors the data that comes into the team, protecting members from information overload and distractions.

You can assign these roles in a number of ways (see chapter 4, "Agree on Individuals' Roles"). You might play to individuals' strengths, asking someone with good interpersonal skills to serve as ambassador, for example. Or you could use the roles to complement the work that members do inside the team. Your team's project manager might act as the task coordinator, since she'd be doing many of those activities anyway.

One team I worked with managed its stakeholders like clients: Individuals "owned" entire relationships and maintained them by taking on multiple roles rather than divvying them among members. For a given stakeholder, the same team member would manage perception of the team (ambassador), make sure the work went smoothly (task coordinator), and inform the team of important challenges its clients faced (scout).

Whatever approach your team chooses, the critical takeaway is this: To succeed internally, it must also succeed externally. By managing the people and groups that will have an impact on your team, you avoid getting blindsided by surprises, gain input into significant decisions, and build a reputation that precedes you in a *good* way.

Section 3
Close Out Your Team

Chapter 14
Deliver the Goods

As your team's work begins to wrap up, you may find yourself starting to mentally and emotionally move on. It's hard *not* to. You're thinking about everything you've put on hold during this project—all the other work that's once again screaming for your attention. Maybe your mind is starting to wander a little in meetings or you're quicker to lose patience with a team member who grates on your nerves. You might be tempted to cut a corner or two just to finish things up.

Chances are, your team members feel the same way. How do you keep everyone, including yourself, focused and working productively so that your team delivers the goods on time and up to quality standards? By devoting as much care to maintaining the relationships as you do to completing the tasks—up until the very end.

Manage Emotions

As your project draws to a close, members may feel fulfilled by a job well done, relieved that the pressure is finally letting up, sad to stop working together, or regretful about conflicts that erupted along the way. They may be anxious about what they'll be doing next or whom they'll report to. Or, after putting in so much hard work, they may worry about passing the baton to others in the organization: What if they ignore the team's recommendations or make ill-considered changes?

Help members deal with the ups and downs by reminding them that closure is imminent. Talk openly, as a group, about how everyone's feeling to signal that those emotions are normal but still need to be managed. Agree on how the team will safeguard against letting emotions compromise the work that remains.

One team leader became very adept at anticipating, recognizing, and dealing with members' feelings. He ran the training program for new hires at a boutique financial firm. Two times a year, he would get a class of about 15 to 20 new hires. In addition to educating them about the company's products, he tried to "mold them into a tight unit." During the six months of training, he encouraged individuals to study together and quiz one another as they prepared for the exam they would take at the end. He knew that their anxiety would dramatically increase as the exam drew near—and that they'd need one another's support as they transitioned from the safe haven of the program to the demanding real world. In the last few weeks, he did weekly assessments with the group, asking questions like these: "On a scale of 1 (terrible) to 10 (great), how are you feeling about exam prep? How are you feeling about starting your 'real' job? How are you feeling about this unit?" As members shared their ratings, he acknowledged their feelings, focusing on what individuals, the team, or he could do to manage them. One outcome from the discussions was a new wiki where people could post questions to the entire group. This not only helped with exam prep but also reminded individuals that they were part of a larger group that would face the exam together.

Orchestrate Your Delivery

A strong handoff is essential to your team's overall success. Otherwise, all the accumulated time and effort is wasted.

Suppose senior executives asked your team to analyze a problem and make a recommendation. Unless members make a solid case for their proposed solution—documenting and presenting their findings in a clear, engaging way—their research and analysis won't amount to anything. Or say the team explored a new product idea and created a prototype. That developed idea won't become a reality unless you get people in manufacturing to buy in to the specifications.

So keep in close contact, as you did in the team's early days, by increasing the number of check-ins and amount of face time. That will keep the energy up and prevent people from taking shortcuts or dropping tasks altogether. One team leader posted a calendar in the office 15 days before the final deadline and, with great flourish, crossed off each passing day. Another held brief "count-down" meetings toward the end. First thing every morning, she assembled her team in the hallway (standing, to signal urgency) and asked members to quickly report on their plans for that day.

Another way to keep people alert is to include them in delivering the end result. It's easy to disengage if you've completed all of your delegated tasks. But if your name is on the final report or you'll participate in the presentation to senior management, you'll stay focused.

And make sure to give your team something to look forward to. Whether you celebrate completion with a dinner out or bring pizza to the last meeting, let people know what you're planning to do. That will give productivity a nice boost as you head to the finish line. It's a way of saying, "Just a *little* more, and we'll be done."

Provide Closure

We have diplomas and graduation ceremonies to mark the end of school, retirement parties to commemorate a career, trophies to recognize our sports achievements. So why don't we close out our teams and projects with some gesture, act, or event? Often, it's because we're busy or we've already leapt to the next team or project. Sometimes we don't want to acknowledge that our work or relationships will end and that change is imminent.

So teams tend to drift apart rather than come to a clear, definitive close. They keep canceling or postponing their increasingly unnecessary meetings. Attendance dwindles, and those who do come get frustrated. And the opportunity to show the team how much you appreciate and respect everyone's effort and time slips away.

Providing closure and wrapping up on a positive note makes members more inclined to join future teams if you invite them. Here are some ways of doing that:

- Hand out awards (humorous or real) that show appreciation for individual contributions.

- Send letters to their managers outlining their contributions, and give copies to your team members so that they can see the accolades.

- Invite senior executives to the final meeting. Have them express their thanks and discuss how the team's work supports the company's strategic priorities.

- Ask team members to talk about which tasks gave them the greatest sense of accomplishment.

- Discuss the team's successes and what could be done better in the future.

That last point is crucial. Don't forget to acknowledge the failures. It's even more important than celebrating the successes. What if senior management rejects the team's recommendations? What if the prototype can't be reproduced on the factory floor? Help members recover, and put them in a constructive frame of mind for the next project. You might, for example, have a champagne toast to the prospect "that got away" or hold a funeral for a proposal that got killed. One engineering team actually filled a box with copies of project-related materials and buried it in a hole behind the company parking lot. Then each member took a moment to reminisce about the project. It added some levity to the situation and put the loss into perspective.

Learning from the past, in preparation for future teams and projects, is your next and final step as a team leader.

Chapter 15
Learn from Your Team's Experiences

Before rushing off to the next big project, reflect on what worked and what didn't for your team. That way, you carry forward processes that served you well and change those that didn't on work with future teams. You don't want to experience déjà vu as the same people create bottlenecks, for example, or the same decision-making processes create "winners" who dominate and "losers" who drag their feet.

As veteran project manager Ray Sheen points out in the *HBR Guide to Project Management*, many organizations provide templates to evaluate the work and the outcomes. You fill out those reports and send them up to senior managers for review, both to inform them about your initiative and to contribute institutional knowledge that will help managers of future projects in their own planning and execution.

For each project you complete, you'll need to evaluate how well the team met its targets (task outcomes, timelines, budgets, resource usage) and analyze the lessons learned at each stage.

You'll also want to conduct an evaluation of people and processes. Do a review at both the team level (rules and processes) and the individual level (behaviors).

Evaluate the Team

When examining the group's performance, pose questions such as:

1. Did we adhere to our rules and processes?

2. Did we achieve our process goals?

3. What factors (planned and unplanned, inside and outside the team) contributed to our success? What got in our way?

4. What did we do well? What should we continue doing on future teams?

5. What did we not do well? What changes should we make going forward?

You can use accountability exercises (see chapter 9, "Hold People Accountable") to facilitate the discussion. Just shift the focus from the here and now ("What can we do better on *this* team?") to future ("What can we do better on our *next* teams?").

Or try this exercise, which highlights personal reactions to the group dynamic: Ask members to reflect on their entire experience working together and share their thoughts with the full team. Here are some questions to consider:

1. What gave you the greatest satisfaction working on this team?

2. What was the most difficult or frustrating aspect?

3. What did you learn about working with others?

4. What did you learn about accomplishing tasks?

5. What would you suggest doing again on future teams? What would you change?

Evaluate Individuals

Next take a look at individual contributions and behaviors. Team members need to know which behaviors they personally should continue and which they should stop or adjust as they move to future teams. Ask members to answer the following two questions about each of their colleagues.

1. How did this person contribute?

2. What could he or she do differently to become an even more valuable team member?

During the team's final feedback session, have members share their comments about one another. And ask someone to take notes so that people can reflect later on what was said.

If your team members have grown skilled at giving and receiving honest feedback, you may want them to conduct a more rigorous review. Have them rate one another on dimensions such as sharing the workload and solving problems, perhaps with the same assessments they used for continuous improvement discussions (see the Process Ratings Exercise in chapter 9) or an abbreviated one, such as the Final Ratings Exercise (see sidebar).

In a growing number of organizations, individuals' compensation depends partly on peer ratings like these. That practice stems from the assumption that peers are in the best position to know how much work employees do and the level of quality they achieve. Though the boss—which may be you, the team leader—will still conduct annual performance appraisals, peer assessments add useful data to the mix. But in my experience, it's best to use them only if you've made that explicit in the original team contract; peer ratings should not be used as a response to uneven work or disruptive behavior. Otherwise, you'll sacrifice the trust you've worked so hard to develop in the group. Ideally, peer ratings are a natural extension of team feedback. If you feel the need to collect them privately to ensure honesty, consider that a red flag, and don't use them. Your team isn't ready.

After members hear their feedback, encourage them to digest it and align their self-perceptions with those of the group. Suggest that they write down what they've learned, what they disagree with, how they feel they've contributed to the team's outcomes and processes, how they may have hindered progress, what they'll do

FINAL RATINGS EXERCISE

Before meeting to discuss individuals' performance, ask people to score each team member on these dimensions (or others the team deems relevant). As individuals share their ratings, they should explain their thinking and offer suggestions for ways their colleagues can improve.

1. Adhered to team rules

1	2	3	4	5	6	7	8	9	10

2. Fully contributed to our process goals and team culture

1	2	3	4	5	6	7	8	9	10

3. Completed tasks on time and with care

1	2	3	4	5	6	7	8	9	10

4. Engaged in and supported team decisions

1	2	3	4	5	6	7	8	9	10

5. Gave and received feedback appropriately

1	2	3	4	5	6	7	8	9	10

6. Resolved conflicts and promoted harmony

1	2	3	4	5	6	7	8	9	10

OVERALL SCORE

1	2	3	4	5	6	7	8	9	10

differently on future teams, and what they'll do to keep developing their team membership skills. They'll be more likely to act on the feedback if you have them process it on their own.

You might also work with individuals to craft a development plan together, if appropriate. Ask members to keep their written reflections as a reminder of what they're committing to do (stop, start, continue) on future teams.

Agree on Principles

These end-of-team discussions and exercises help provide closure. They also wipe the slate clean for the next team experience. Often the conversations are cathartic, helping people move beyond grudges or perceived injuries and prime them for a fresh start.

Make your final review as productive as possible by:

- **Agreeing up front how you'll handle it.** This is your last conversation about accountability. It will go much more smoothly—and people will get more out of it—if the team has decided earlier, in discussions about rules and processes, what will happen at this stage. Members need to know in advance how they'll be held accountable along the way *and* at the end so that they can monitor their behavior accordingly. Nothing is more demoralizing than being critiqued for something without receiving fair warning.

- **Giving people time to consider what they will say.** People should avoid speaking off the cuff, especially when delivering feedback to individual members.

- **Providing guidance on what to say and how to say it.** Regarding the "what," remind everyone that this conversation is about the future. The final review is *not* the time to rehash past mistakes or bring up new pain points. Instead, it's a chance to acknowledge what people (as a team and as individuals) did well and should continue on future teams, and what they could do differently to improve the next team experience. Regarding the "how," remind members of the team's feedback and accountability rules (see chapters 5 and 6), and ask them to frame their comments constructively.

Since the beginning, you've led your team through continuous improvement: You established goals, roles, and rules; helped members build essential team skills; and held them accountable to the contract they agreed on. Now, at the end, you're identifying best practices for the future.

The final review promotes learning and improvement *across* teams: Individuals hone their team behaviors into even more productive ones; you sharpen your leadership skills; and future teams benefit from the growth all around.

Appendix A
Rules Inventory

This exercise provides structure for a team conversation about desired behaviors, or rules of conduct. Under each category, you'll find open questions to help identify rules the team may already be following, followed by prompts for considering new ones. If you're leading a new team, you might revise the open questions and ask people what has worked well (or not) for them on previous teams.

	Do Now	Add
RESPECT AND TRUST		
What do we do well? What might we do differently?		
Keep conversations confidential.		
Be punctual.		
Return phone calls and e-mails by close of business each day.		
Avoid sarcasm, snide remarks, or melodramatic body language (such as eye rolling) when conveying disagreement.		
Don't sulk or give the silent treatment when your position has not prevailed.		
Respect other people's ways of accomplishing tasks; don't redo work or impose your way on others.		
Be flexible.		
Listen without interpreting people's motives. Ask why they said, did, or asked for something.		
Volunteer to take on work when you can without doing the "who's doing more/less" calculation.		
Other:		

NORMS

	Do Now	Add
MEETING DISCUSSIONS/ DECISION MAKING		
What do we do well? What might we do differently?		
Share "airtime," listen, and don't interrupt others.		
Invite quiet people to speak.		
Resist regarding an opposing view as a personal affront.		
Be willing to change your position or compromise.		
Support the team's final decision, even when it's different from the one you proposed.		
Stop advocating your position after a decision has been made.		
Make sure people have been given the floor to present their views before a decision is made.		
Other:		

(*continued*)

(continued)

	Do Now	Add
DISSENT AND INNOVATION		
What do we do well? What might we do differently?		
Rigorously examine multiple options, and their respective strengths and weaknesses, before evaluating alternatives and making decisions.		
Protect dissenting views by encouraging the speaker to explain and preventing others from immediately dismissing the ideas.		
Encourage innovation by delaying evaluation.		
Reframe "This will never work" as "How could we make it work?"		
Other:		

	Do Now	Add
FEEDBACK AND REPORTING		
What do we do well? What might we do differently?		
Give the team status updates according to the prescribed process (which the team determines).		
Give a "heads-up" and be responsible for the consequences if you have to miss a deadline.		
Give positive feedback frequently; speak up when someone's behavior helps the team.		
Give negative feedback constructively. State the observed behavior and its impact on the team, ask for the other person's perceptions, and suggest a preferred behavior.		
Admit your own mistakes.		
Listen and avoid defensiveness when receiving constructive feedback.		
When giving or receiving feedback, put it in the context of helping the team move toward its goals.		
Other:		

(continued)

Appendix A

(continued)

	Do Now	Add
CONFLICT RESOLUTION		
What do we do well? What might we do differently?		
Assume that every team member is working in good faith toward the team's goals.		
Put conflict "on the table" for discussion.		
Discuss conflict with the goal of identifying what is best for the team's future.		
Discuss the conflict first with the person involved; avoid talking behind anyone's back.		
Don't yell, use profanity, make threats, or walk out of discussions.		
Other:		

Appendix B
Cultural Audit

Ask team members to describe the group's way of operating, as if you were bringing someone new onboard. Have them quickly answer the following questions, without overthinking their responses.

What would you tell new team members about how we:

Communicate

- How do we share information? (Through what channels? What's the tone and level of formality?)

- Who can—or can't—we communicate with? What chain of command do we need to honor?

- What's the expected response time? Is it ever OK to be "offline"? If so, when, and how do we inform others of our availability?

- What are the standards for presentations?

- What are the standards for written documents?

Conduct meetings

- How do we run meetings? How long are they? How frequent? What's the tone and level of formality?

- Why do we hold meetings?

- Who should attend? When is it OK to meet in subgroups, and when is the full team required? How and when do we invite outsiders?

- How do we handle sensitive or confidential issues?

Make decisions

- What is our process for making decisions?

- Who makes them? Who is included and who isn't?

- How do we communicate decisions? Who gets told about them? Through what medium? What's the tone and level of formality?

Handle differing viewpoints

- How do we solicit dissent (if at all)? At meetings? In e-mail? One-on-one?

- How do people offer dissenting ideas or opinions? How direct should the language be?

- Is dissent allowed from everyone?

- Are some people never to be challenged?

Delegate work

- How do we negotiate timelines and resources (if at all)?

- How do we communicate assignments? (Through what medium? At what level of detail? What's the tone and level of formality?)

- How do we make sure that all team members understand their roles?

- How do we reach agreement on outcomes and schedules?

- How do people get feedback on their tasks?

Manage projects

- How do we keep teammates and stakeholders up to date on progress? (Through scheduled status reports? When things go wrong? At project milestones?)

- Who gets told? How frequently?

- What's included?

- What happens with problems, missed deadlines, changes, adjustments, and so on? How do we communicate them? How do we get back on track?

Appendix C
Team Contract

Here's a template for capturing the goals, roles, rules, and metrics your team has agreed to. Update your contract periodically, as members, tasks, and timelines change.

Brief team description:

Date:

Team members:

Name	Contact information	Signature

Goals that will serve as a unifying force in the work ahead:

Task goals (what we'll accomplish)
Process goals (how we'll work together)

Roles we've identified to ensure performance:

Roles	Names

Rules of conduct:

Meetings	
Communication	
Decision making	
Managing tasks	
Managing relationships	

Evaluation plan (how we'll determine that we've achieved our goals):

Index

accountability, 55–65, 87–97
achievements
  celebrating, 58–59, 137
  early, 126–127
  See also recognition
activity, defining roles by, 36,
  40–42
advocacy groups, 83–84, 96
ambassador, team, 129, 130. *See*
  also roles
anger, handling, 105. *See also*
  emotions, managing;
  conflicts
Artifact Exercise, 14–15, 110
assessments
  of individual performance,
  141–144
  personality, allaying fears
  about, 20–23
  of personality and work style,
  17–19
  of team performance, 140–141
audit, cultural, 51–54, 153–156
autonomy, 42–43

behavior. *See* conduct, rules of
boundary
  individual, 42–43
  management of, 123–130
  roles, 128–130
buy-in, for decisions, 76

closure, providing, 136–138
collaboration, 8, 99. *See also* rules
  of conduct
communication
  outside of team, 126
  team (*see* rules of conduct;
  feedback)
concerns of team members,
  32–33. *See also* goals
conduct, rules of, 45–54, 74,
  108–109
conflicts
  dissent and, 81–85
  reasons for, 103–107
  reframing, 111–114
  resolving, 103–116
  truths about, 112–113
  unresolved, 112–113
consensus building, 75, 77. *See*
  also decision making
continuous improvement, 58, 59,
  114–115, 145
contract, team, 67–69, 157–159
creativity, in decision making,
  76–77. *See also* decision
  making
culture, team, 28–29
cultural audit, 51–54, 153–156

deadlines, 27
debriefing, 59–60, 139–145

decision making
  buy-in, 76
  by consensus, 75, 77
  context for, 75–78
  creativity and, 76
  criteria for, 74–75
  dissent and, 81–85
  expert opinions and, 76,
    80–81
  group, 25–26
  as growth opportunity, 76
  individual, 26
  by majority vote, 77
  nominal method of, 49–51
  participation in, 78–80
  team, 73–85
  timing and, 75
deliverables, 133–145. *See also*
  goals
devil's advocate role, 41, 84–85
disagreements, 103–116. *See also*
  conflicts
DISC assessment, 18. *See also*
  personality traits
discussion. *See* communication
dissent, 81–85, 104. *See also*
  conflicts
diversity
  in teams, 3–6
  of work styles, 8–10
dysfunction. *See* conflicts

emotions, managing, 134–135
empathy, in conflict resolution,
  110–111
evaluations, 139–145
exercises
  artifact, 14–15, 110
  final ratings, 142, 143
  process ratings, 89–91, 142
  stop-start-continue,
    92–93
expectations, defining, 39. *See*
  also rules of conduct
experiences, learning from,
  139–145
expertise, 7–8, 36, 76, 80–81
external value, 127–128. *See also*
  boundary management

failures, acknowledging, 137–138
fairness, 99. *See also* rules of
  conduct
feedback, 55–65, 87–94, 101,
  141–144
Final Ratings Exercise, 142, 143.
  See also evaluations
final review, 139–145
functional groups, 124. *See also*
  stakeholders
future, envisioning, and conflict
  resolution, 114–116

goals
  conflicts about, 106–107
  establishing, 25–34
  importance of, 25–26
  personal, 29–30
  process, 25, 28–33
  task, 25, 26–28
group decision making, 25–26,
  73–85
group feedback, 94. *See also*
  feedback
groupthink, 82. *See also*
  diversity
guard, team, 129. *See also*
  roles

hopes, of team members,
  32–33. *See also* goals
hurt feelings, 105. *See also*
  emotions, managing;
  conflicts

ideals, of team members, 32.
  See also goals
individuals
  evaluating, 141–144
  interests of, reconciling with
    team interests, 42–43
  recognition of, 99–102
information flow, 126
introductions, 11–15, 120
inward information flow
  management, 129–130

knowledge, of team members,
  7–8

launch meetings, 11–24
law of reciprocity, 127–128
leaders
    of other teams, 124 (*see also*
        stakeholders)
    roles of, 37–40
learning, 139–145

majority vote, 77. *See also*
    decision making
metrics, 27–28. *See also* goals
multiple intelligences, 18. *See
    also* personality traits
Myers-Briggs Type Indicator, 17,
    18, 120. *See also* personality
    traits

negative feedback, 56–57, 60–65.
    See also feedback
new members, welcoming,
    117–121
nominal method of decision
    making, 49–51
norms. *See* rules of conduct

optimal decisions, 73–85
outcomes. *See* goals
outward information flow
    management, 129

peer ratings, 142. *See also*
    evaluations
personal goals, 29–30
personality traits, 17–19, 31, 40,
    120–121
personal strengths, 13–15,
    109–110
perspectives
    opposing, 104
    variety of, 5–6
positive feedback, 56–57, 61, 101.
    See also feedback
priorities of team members, 19,
    23–24
problem solving. *See* conflicts;
    decision making
process goals, 25, 28–33
Process Ratings Exercise, 89–91,
    142

process roles, 40–41. *See also*
    roles
public credit, 101–102. *See also*
    successes

reciprocity, law of, 127–128
recognition, 99–102
reputation, establishing your
    team's, 125–127
roles
    by activity, 36, 40–42
    ambassador, 129, 130
    boundary, 128–130
    defining by structure, 36,
        37–40
    defining by task, 40–41
    devil's advocate, 84–85
    establishing, 35–43
    goal/rule keeper, 41, 60
    guard, 129
    leader, 37–40
    process, 40–41
    scout, 129–130
    by structure, 36, 37–40
    task, 40–41
    task coordinator, 128, 130
rules inventory, 147–152
rules of conduct, 45–54, 74,
    108–109

scout, team, 129–130. *See also* roles
senior managers, 124, 125, 126.
    See also stakeholders
skills, of team members, 7–8
stakeholders, 124–125
stop-start-continue exercise,
    92–94
structure, defining roles by, 36,
    37–40
subject-matter experts, 80–81
successes
    celebrating, 58–59, 137
    early, 126–127

task
    coordinator, team, 128, 130 (*see
    also* roles)
    goals, 25, 26–28
    roles, 40–41

Index

team members
  accountability of, 55–65, 87–97
  behaviors of, 37–38
  connecting with, one-on-one,
    100
  contributions by, 78–80
  departing, 119
  development of, 76
  difficult, 3–4
  diversity in, 3–6, 8–10
  evaluating, 8, 141–144
  existing, 7
  expectations of, 39
  expertise of, 7–8, 36, 76, 80–81
  fears about assessment of,
    20–23
  introductions, 11–15, 120
  managing emotions of,
    134–135
  negative behavior by, 56–57
  nonproductive, 95–97
  personal strengths of, 13–15,
    109–110
  priorities of, 19, 23–24
  recognition of, 99–102
  reconciling individual and
    team interests, 42–43
  relationships among, xii
  roles of, 35–43
  rules of conduct for, 45–54
  selecting, 3–10
  welcoming new, 117–121
  work styles of, 8–10, 16–19,
    103–104, 120–121

teams
  accountability, 87–92
  building winning, 3–10
  closing out, xiv–xv, 133–145
  conflict resolution on,
    103–116
  contract, 67–69, 157–159
  culture, 28–29
  delivery of goods by, 133–138
  evaluating, 140–141
  goals for, 25–34, 106–107
  infrastructure, xiii, 73
  launch meetings for, 11–24
  learning from experiences of,
    139–145
  management, xiii–xiv
  managing outside of,
    123–130
  reconciling individual and
    team interests, 42–43
  reputation of, 125–127
  rules of conduct for, 45–54,
    74, 108–109
  size, 7
  trust, xii. *See also* rules of
    conduct
two-way information flow,
    managing, 128

work styles, 8–10, 16–19, 103–
    104, 120–121
wrap-up meeting, 59–60, 137,
    144–145

About the Author

Mary Shapiro has worked with *Fortune* 500 companies, nonprofit organizations, and government agencies as a consultant and executive trainer for more than 20 years. She has developed and delivered executive education programs at Simmons College since 1988 and joined the Simmons MBA faculty in 1993. She holds the Trust Professorship of Leadership Development at Simmons College School of Management. Shapiro specializes in four areas: team building and intervention, communicating in a diverse and virtual environment, personal effectiveness in influence and motivation, and strategic career management.

Notes

Notes

Notes

Notes

Notes

Notes

Notes

Notes

Notes

 Leading Teams

Now that you've completed the *HBR Guide to Leading Teams*, get your team performing at peak efficiency with the **HBR Guide to Leading Teams Ebook + Tools**.

This digital product, available exclusively at hbr.org, will help you put the ideas from the book into action and focus on improving your team with 14 ready-to-use, customizable digital tools including:

→ **Leader's Manual** to guide you through every exercise—its goal and purpose, when to do it, how you know when you're done, and what to do next

→ **Leader's Inventory Form** to help you pick the right people for the job

→ **Cultural Audit** to promote harmony among team members

→ **Rules of Conduct Inventory** to ensure a shared understanding of expectations

→ **Team Formation Log and Worksheet** to build a solid foundation for your team

→ **Peer Feedback Forms** to foster productive critique and cooperation

Available for just $39.95, the HBR Guide to Leading Teams Ebook + Tools may be the most important investment in your team's success you'll ever make.

 Harvard Business Review Press